MORE
What Do I
Do Whe...

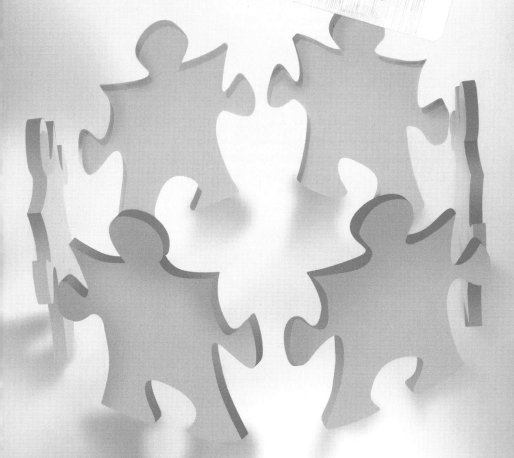

Powerful Strategies to
Promote Positive Behavior

Allen N. Mendler

Solution Tree

Origi...

Originally published as *Just in Time: Powerful Strategies to Promote
Positive Behavior*. Copyright © 2005 by Solution Tree
(formerly National Educational Service).

Cover design by Grannan Design, Ltd.
Art by Barbara Murray Sullivan

Printed in the United States of America

ISBN: 978-1-934009-08-6

*To the memory of my parents, Harold and Ida Mendler,
who raised me with discipline and dignity. And to my sister and
brother, Andrea Yekutiel and Scott Mendler, with whom
I have shared so many meaningful life events.*

Acknowledgments

I am grateful to the numerous educators throughout the country who shared their stories and strategies that made this book possible. I have been blessed with the good fortune of having had many opportunities to share my knowledge with you and to learn so much from you that I can pass along to others. I have found that there is always a wealth of untapped great ideas among faculty in every school, yet these ideas too often go unshared due to various constraints. Much of my work involves helping educators share their best ideas with each other. My hope is that *MORE What Do I Do When . . . ? Powerful Strategies to Promote Positive Behavior* will help make life a bit easier for educators by enhancing the success and improving the behavior of our students.

A special thanks to my son Brian Mendler, a youthful yet wise special-education teacher and outstanding Discipline With Dignity presenter whose dedication to making life better for his challenging students has had a dramatic impact on many of their lives. I thank Brian for his editorial comments and for contributing his "legacy" strategy. In addition to Brian, I thank my wife, Barbara, who recently retired from a lengthy career in education. At her retirement dinner, one speaker after another referred to her as always being "all about the kids." Wonderfully, she has also always found the time and energy to be there for our family and for me. Our lengthy talks about kids and schools have shaped much of my thinking over the years.

I want to give special thanks to my editors at Solution Tree for their fine work. I also wish to acknowledge Carolyn Pool, acquisitions editor at ASCD, for enthusiastically embracing this book in its earliest form. I also wish to acknowledge Lori Erickson and all the folks at the Otter Creek Institute for their support of my work and their flexibility in allowing me to schedule seminars that fit my life. My program manager at Discipline Associates, Tammy Rowland, deserves special mention due to her excellence at keeping Discipline Associates well-organized. Our primary associates—Willeta Corbett, Jerry Evanski, Brian Mendler, Dave Zawadzki, and Colleen Zawadzki—deserve special mention for the fine work they do in teaching discipline seminars to educators throughout the country. Finally, and as always, a particularly special acknowledgment of my partner, frequent coauthor, and best friend, Rick Curwin, for his constant optimism, great sense of humor, and love.

Contents

Table of Contents

About the Author

Allen N. Mendler, Ph.D., is an educator, school psychologist, and the parent of three children. He has worked extensively with children of all ages in regular education and special-education settings. Dr. Mendler has consulted in many schools and in day and residential centers, including extensive work with youth in juvenile detention. Dr. Mendler's emphasis is on developing effective frameworks and strategies for educators, youth professionals, and parents to help difficult youth succeed. As one of the internationally acclaimed authors of *Discipline With Dignity*, Dr. Mendler has given many workshops and seminars to professionals and parents, and is highly acclaimed as a motivational speaker and trainer for numerous educational organizations.

Dr. Mendler is the author or coauthor of several books, including *As Tough As Necessary, What Do I Do When . . . ? How to Achieve Discipline With Dignity in the Classroom,* and *Power Struggles: Successful Techniques for Educators.* His book *Connecting With Students* provides numerous practical strategies that help educators connect with even their most difficult students. His articles have appeared in many journals, including *Educational Leadership, Kappan, Learning, Reclaiming*

Children and Youth, and *Reaching Today's Youth.* Dr. Mendler has been recognized for his distinguished teaching, and was a recipient of the coveted Crazy Horse Award for having made outstanding contributions to discouraged youth. He lives with his family in Rochester, New York.

He is cofounder of Discipline Associates, which provides training and staff development to educators and youth providers in the areas of behavior management and motivation.

Introduction

Chad no longer does any of the classwork that he finds boring. Beth complains endlessly, talks to peers constantly, and is forever asking irrelevant questions. When upset, Luis curls up under his desk and starts kicking it or makes noises. Rachelle picks at her arm until it bleeds and pierces her ears and lips in class. Bob often draws on himself and frequently sleeps in class.

Is it any wonder that most educators are exasperated as they try to simultaneously raise academic achievement while having to deal with unruly, disruptive behavior? A May 2004 study by Public Agenda found that more than one in three teachers said they either have seriously thought about leaving teaching because they are tired of dealing with behavior problems or know a teacher who has quit for that reason. *MORE What Do I Do When . . . ? Powerful Strategies to Promote Positive Behavior* addresses the need for strategies to effectively handle challenging students.

Several years ago, Rick Curwin and I wrote *Discipline With Dignity* (Curwin & Mendler, 1988, 1999), which set forth an approach to school and classroom discipline focusing on personal responsibility and shared community as the foundation upon which all successful strategies reside. The revised 1999 edition of our book reaffirmed its present relevance, despite the passage of years. Our goal was to provide educators with the information needed to deal both effectively and humanely with children, while showing how enhancing and preserving a child's dignity along with providing a sense of hope are always essential. We highlighted the differences between methods of obedience with those of responsibility; illustrated the power of eliciting good behavior through increased student involvement; showed the relationships among stress, motivation, teaching methods, and discipline problems; and offered alternatives to lose-lose power struggles.

In 1992, I wrote *What Do I Do When . . . ? How to Achieve Discipline With Dignity in the Classroom,* emphasizing that an understanding of the basic needs that drive student misbehavior is a key to identifying effective strategies of prevention and intervention. Our book, *As Tough as Necessary: A Discipline With Dignity Approach to Countering Aggression, Hostility, and Violence* (Curwin & Mendler, 1997) provides strategies for interacting effectively with students who are hostile, aggressive, or violent. *Discipline With Dignity for Challenging Youth* (Mendler & Curwin, 1999, 2007) shows how to effectively work with especially difficult youth. All of these comprehensive texts present and discuss the many facets of in-school and out-of-school life that converge to create discipline problems. In addition, these books offer the framework that serves as the foundation upon which schools and classroom teachers can develop all-inclusive discipline programs that work. The reception among educators to our efforts has been phenomenally uplifting while simultaneously humbling. The daily testimonials of appreciation we hear from fellow educators who thank us for "all we have done" resonate against the backdrop of all that still needs to be done. Evans (2002) recently reminded us that "what has changed over the last thirty years is not the skills of our teachers but rather the lives of our students."

Introduction

We are all extremely busy, and there are too many demands placed upon us (some of them ridiculous). As educators, we are expected to meet the academic needs of behaviorally diverse students, many lacking parental nurturance, some without a roof over their heads, and more than a few wearing labels and acronyms such as *oppositional defiant, attention-deficit, autistic, EBD* (emotional-behavior disorder), *LD* (learning disability), *SBD* (severe behavior disorder), and *OCD* (obsessive-compulsive disorder). These students present instructional and behavioral challenges never before *tolerated* in mainstream school settings. Therefore, as educators we can continue to do what we have always done and hope that somehow things will get better, or we can adapt with the times and implement strategies in our classrooms that are likely to get better results. The very essence of *MORE What Do I Do When . . . ? Powerful Strategies to Promote Positive Behavior* is an ample supply of strategies for handling a wide variety of challenging situations that virtually every educator will face. This book provides proven ways for dealing effectively with misbehavior, while focusing on ways to meet the daunting task of creating and sustaining an effective learning climate that promotes positive behavior.

The primary goal is to offer educators who are pressed for time a practical, easy-to-read book of specific strategies that offers resource methods of *prevention* and *intervention. MORE What Do I Do When . . . ?* is a hybrid resource in that it presents some of the most effective strategies first identified in *What Do I Do When . . . ?* and our other books, along with new approaches that have been shared and developed by many educators throughout the country. Although there is no substitute for comprehensive, theoretically sound texts that also offer practical advice, this book of tips is designed to give busy educators many specific methods that motivate students and prevent discipline problems from happening and effective interventions that *stop misbehavior* while preserving everyone's dignity.

EIGHT UNDERLYING PRINCIPLES

Eight basic principles and beliefs are at the core of good methods of discipline. Discipline With Dignity prides itself on being a philosophy that can cultivate a lot of different strategies. Not all strategies work for all people because the personality and style of the person using the strategy will determine its effectiveness—at least as much as the strategy itself. Two teachers can use the same words to tell a student to sit down and have very different results. While strategies may need to vary, the basic elements that underlie all strategies can serve as a framework for all educators. Just as we know that nutrients and water are necessities for all living things to grow and flourish, there are certain ingredients that all good methods of discipline must have in order to succeed. Although *MORE What Do I Do When . . . ?* is a hands-on, practical guide of tips to help with a variety of school behavior problems, we begin with the following eight principles that form the foundation for the strategies in this book.

Principle 1: Discipline Is Everyone's Job

I have attended several suspension hearings in my career. Although a viable alternative to suspension may not always be feasible, every time a student is suspended the school gives up all control over that student's whereabouts and behavior. Because we are all busy, it may be easy for us to dismiss the student's absence as "not our problem." In fact, many of us feel relieved that the student's absence has reduced our level of stress. But if the suspended student is not in school, there is a very good chance that he is out in the community idling the time away. What was a school problem can quickly become a community problem. Even worse, we could become a target if the student decides to fill vacant time by breaking into unoccupied homes. Certainly, the student expelled from my school knows where I am during the day, making my house an easy target.

There is no question that at least 70 to 80% of school disciplinary problems have their roots in factors outside of school. Certainly student behavior in school would improve immensely if more parents did their jobs properly, if poverty vanished, if drugs were eradicated, and if violence disappeared. As educators, our voice accounts for no more than 20 to 30% of what kids hear and understand. It is imperative that all adults in the school community see themselves as players in the process of influencing change. As educators, we need to feel confident and empowered in our skills to handle inappropriate behavior. We are all stakeholders when it comes to the effects of student behavior.

Principle 2: Good Discipline Is About Teaching Better Behavior, Not Just Offering "Quick Fixes"

Effective, long-term resolution of disciplinary problems takes time. Although it is understandable to want a quick fix, misbehaving students are telling us that something important in their lives is keeping them from being fully with us. For some, it is their belief that they are too stupid to succeed, while others know no way other than to bully in order to feel in charge. Some act out to mask depression, while others seek affiliation, attention, or recognition. Essentially, kids who misbehave are telling us that their basic needs are not being met. Although we need to have specific, short-term strategies to handle inappropriate behavior, good discipline is linked to our understanding of the motives that drive students to act inappropriately and the solutions that address these basic needs. When students behave badly, we need to ask ourselves why they find it more preferable to act inappropriately. In essence, students need to feel connected, competent, and influential. If they do not, they are likely to respond with maladaptive behavior. Attention-seekers generally have an overriding need to belong and be viewed as important by others. Students who do not believe they are capable either give up on school and act unmotivated or misbehave when required to do something that they view as overwhelming. Students who are aggressive or disrespectful are usually trying to influence the world around them. In order to teach better behavior, one needs to factor in the motives that drive poor behavior. As Glasser (1986) noted, discipline problems are resolved when schools become "needs-satisfying" places. Many strategies can help us achieve this goal.

Principle 3: The Relationships We Have With Students Are Inextricably Linked to Our Effectiveness With Discipline

Sandy Melton, a teacher in Corpus Christi, Texas, shares her experience in teaching Manuel, a boy from the barrio, who sat in the back of her fifth-period class. Manuel was so disruptive with his antics that he prevented most of the class from paying attention to their assignments:

> He wore a blue bandana and delighted in receiving attention and gaining control. As was my custom when he started disrupting my class, I informed him that he had a detention, which didn't bother him at all. . . . I think he had gotten used to having an eighth-period class called detention, and we got to know each other quite well during these additional hours together. At one point he told me he wasn't going to amount to anything, and everybody knew it. He knew it and his family knew it: He had never done anything good and felt he didn't stand a chance. After several days, Manuel said, "If you will not make me stay for detention tomorrow, I will straighten up, I promise. Will you give me a chance?" Manuel started staying after school on his own, helping me make bulletin boards and grade papers. He loved it when I asked him to be in charge of detention when I left the room, and I would always put him in charge of watching my purse. Remember, this is the kid who at the beginning of the year had stolen calculators, quarters,

hall passes: You name it, he stole it. . . . Next Manuel
wanted to stay after school and started to do his work.
He asked me to teach him to multiply and divide. He
couldn't keep up with everything the class was doing, but
you better believe he passed those 6 weeks. Manuel was a
migrant student and therefore was gone the last 6 weeks
of the year. It blew my mind when he asked for all the
work he would miss so that he could get a grade rather
than another incomplete. . . . This was during my third
year as a teacher, and I know I made mistakes, but I will
always believe that I made a difference in Manuel's life.

As educators and administrators, we must believe we effectively
influence change in the lives of the students we touch. It is imperative
to approach each day as if it is *the day* a breakthrough will happen. An
important part of our job is to believe that today, the student with a
history of disrespectful language will finally share her disagreement in
a more respectful way. We have to act as if a continually disruptive student who is out of his seat every other minute is *today* going to sit still
longer. Working with tough kids requires persistence and optimism. If
we surrender our optimism, it becomes virtually impossible to influence change. At the same time, we must realize that for every three
steps forward we take, there will be two steps back. Virtually all people
revert to their old behaviors several times as they acquire new ones.

Principle 4: Emphasize Strategies That Teach Responsibility

The keys to responsible behavior are to:

- Understand and be aware of what we are doing.
- Predict how our behavior will affect ourselves and others.
- Make adequate and responsible choices.
- Know how consequences are linked to the choices we make.
- Develop good planning skills.

Although obedience-based methods of discipline are preferable to chaos, the best discipline occurs when students internalize the message: This is responsibility-based discipline. Responsibility-based discipline seeks to have students behave well not just when the voice of authority speaks, but also in the absence of authority. By contrast, obedience means "do as you are told" and requires the presence of authority to enforce rules. The major tools of obedience-based discipline are rewards and punishments.

The goal in achieving good discipline should be for students to act appropriately because it is the proper thing to do, rather than acting appropriately out of fear that someone will punish them if they misbehave. Obedience is especially desirable in matters of health and safety. Rewards and punishments are often required in the early stages of development for children to feel a sense of safety and security. But when applied to most misbehavior, such methods are rarely more than short-term solutions that often provoke rebellion among challenging students. Responsibility involves the cognitive process of "making the best decision possible." This occurs more slowly than obedience because it requires providing students with opportunities to sort out facts, make decisions, link consequences with actions, and become more adept at planning. For some, learning responsibility is even more basic—it is about helping them notice how they are currently behaving so that they can take charge of what they do. There appear to be increasing numbers of students who seem to have a disconnection between their brain and their behavior. For these students, inappropriate behavior such as tapping a pencil, getting out of a seat, or talking to a neighbor has become so automatic that there is little if any self-awareness. Responsibility is about helping students make these connections.

Principle 5: We Can Be on the Same Page Without Always Doing the Same Thing

Teaching children to be responsible involves tailoring the consequences for misbehavior to each individual child. Children must be shown and taught the difference between being fair and treating everyone exactly the same. Not all students react the same way to the same consequence, and not all teachers and administrators react the same way to each infraction. Unfortunately, when some educators try to do what they think is right rather than treating everyone the same way, they can be accused of playing favorites and being unfair by other students or their parents. We believe that being fair requires having rules and procedures based on sound values for everyone. When rules are broken, fairness requires the implementation of specific consequences that are most likely to help each particular student improve his or her behavior. Having more than one consequence available enables the teacher to select one that will likely be most effective for the particular student. It should be based on what the educator believes will best help that student learn better behavior. Good discipline requires predictability and flexibility. In school, being fair means giving each person what is needed to be successful and to learn responsibility.

Principle 6: Good Discipline Is Not Just Procedures, Rules, and Consequences: It Is a Vision Guided by Educational Goals and Grounded in Values and Principles

Rules viewed as "stupid" are unlikely to be followed, especially among students who have little interest or incentive for being compliant. In order for rules to work they must make sense, and in order for them to make sense they need to be tied to a value or principle—that is, the purpose served by the rule. Rules are about treating each other in ways that permit learning to take place. For students, rules should provide guidelines for defining *what* we are expected to do and *how* to make it happen. Values relate to the reasons why we treat people the way we do, and they are necessarily general and broad in scope. Values provide students with an answer to *why* they are expected to follow the rules. In the educational environment it is important that the values we emphasize most are those that affect teaching and learning in a positive way. An example of a value is "students should be and feel safe at all times." This is a value because learning cannot successfully take place in an environment where students feel in danger and cannot give attention to their work. Another value, "racism, bigotry, sexism, and anti–any group–ism are not welcome," supports rules that protect students from harassment because a harassed student is unable to learn to his or her full potential. Our schools must define their larger purpose or vision and then settle upon the values that are inherent in accomplishing that vision. Rules and procedures are the specific requirements that characterize proper behavior. We must ask ourselves what we need in our classrooms and schools to ensure that maximum teaching and learning occur. Each teacher must know the values he or she needs to promote in order for teaching and learning to occur in the classroom. Classroom rules and procedures should then be tied directly to those values.

Principle 7: We Have the Most Control Over Our Own Behavior, So We Must Set an Example by Reflecting the Type of Behavior We Expect From Students

Let students see us living by the same code of behavior we expect from them. When assigning homework, we need to promptly do our own homework by returning their work to them as quickly as possible. If we want students to be there for each other, we need to be visible in the halls and make sure that they see us being there for them. If we really want students to learn responsibility, we need to show them that we trust their abilities to make some of the key classroom decisions. When conflict occurs, let them see us implement solutions that are respectful, nonviolent, and verbally nonaggressive. To promote friendliness, we need to have a smile on our face as we greet them into the room. When students show us disrespect and make us angry, we need to show them how to express disapproval firmly, yet with dignity. It can be powerful for students to see us as capable and strong without being brutal when our well-being or their well-being is threatened. We need to expect at least as much of ourselves as we do of them. We need to be ready to teach when the bell rings, know our stuff, and show the same kind of enthusiasm we would like to see from them. Let them see us as a model of how we want them to be. We gain credibility with our students by "walking the talk."

Principle 8: Treat Ourselves, Other Educators, Parents, and Students With Respect and Dignity

It is difficult to be dignified with students who are offensive, disobedient, unmotivated, and intimidating. However, if we submit to the impulse to attack or run away, we lose the opportunity to demonstrate how to effectively manage challenging behavior. As noted above, we only gain credibility when students see us "walking the talk." Showing aggression toward students rarely succeeds in getting them to follow the rules, and virtually always increases the risk of losing them to anger and resentment. A simple test to determine dignity is to imagine being at the receiving end of any method of discipline or correction. For example, how would you feel if your principal forced you to publicly apologize for missing a meeting or wrote your name with a checkmark next to it during a faculty meeting for "off-task" talking? It is important to ask if personal dignity would be assailed or left intact if someone applied the same method on us to influence our behavior. Ways of communicating dignity to our students include listening to what students think, encouraging their feedback, using "I" messages to communicate our feelings to them, apologizing after acting in a hurtful way, explaining why we want something done a certain way and how that will likely be of benefit to your students, and giving them some voice in classroom affairs. The message we want to convey is: *We value who you are. If you behave in an unacceptable way you will be treated in a firm, respectful manner, and you will be held accountable for your actions.*

HOW TO EFFECTIVELY USE THIS BOOK

MORE What Do I Do When . . . ? provides practical, specific tips for discipline prevention and intervention. Use the strategies as described or modify them to more closely fit your situation, keeping in mind that not all strategies work with all students. There is not a "one size fits all method" to fix all behavior problems. You can use the principles in this book as a framework to help you develop new methods. You are likely to improve classroom discipline if you allow your interactive moments and classroom structure to be guided by those principles. In an effort to make *MORE What Do I Do When . . . ?* as user-friendly as possible, the tips on prevention are grouped into four categories:

- Tips for welcoming students
- Tips for establishing effective rules and consequences
- Tips for promoting responsibility and problem-solving methods
- Tips for motivating students

The tips for intervention are grouped into three categories:

- Tips for handling tough moments
- Tips for handling difficult situations
- Tips for helping students handle tough moments and difficult situations

The concluding section of this book consists of frequently asked questions and answers on classroom behavior and provides practical and resourceful tips for handling specific problems and circumstances.

Part 1

Prevention, Intervention, and Choosing a Discipline Method

1 Introduction to Strategies

Managing student behavior . . . is a delicate balance between maintaining social order and meeting the unique needs of each student.

—Richard Curwin and Allen Mendler
(*Discipline With Dignity,* 1988, 1999)

In the original *Discipline With Dignity* (Curwin & Mendler, 1988, 1999), a "three dimensional discipline" model was presented with three components: *prevention, action,* and *resolution.* We suggested numerous ways to *prevent* problems from occurring, to *act* when problems occur, and to *resolve issues* with more challenging students. In daily classroom life, two types of strategies make for effective discipline—prevention and intervention. Prevention involves understanding why students behave inappropriately and then doing things to prevent problems. After problems occur, prevention is also concerned with what can be done to keep the same thing from happening again. Intervention involves stopping misbehavior quickly so that little precious time is lost to instruction. The strategies offered here are with the rubric of prevention and intervention.

PREVENTION

The vast majority of factors leading to chronic discipline problems have their roots outside of school. Dysfunctional families, unsupportive parents, violence in our culture, media messages, drugs, exposure to toxic substances, lack of community support for educational goals, and preoccupation with survival issues are among the many sociocultural factors at the core of most discipline problems. As educators we have little, if any, control over these factors. The foremost tool of prevention we have is ourselves, because despite all of these negative factors, we can and often do make differences in the lives of our students. I frequently say in seminars that our challenge is to make our voice as interesting, harmonious, and inviting as we can because all kinds of factors compete for the hearts, minds, and souls of our students. The daily challenge is to make our voice stand out from the crowd.

Discipline prevention is less about addressing the out-of-school causes of poor behavior and more about addressing basic human needs, which when neglected lead to problem behavior. It might help to think of one of your former students who struggled behaviorally, was troubling to you, showed improvement, and eventually turned out all right. What kinds of things did you do? Why do you think changes occurred? As detailed in *What Do I Do When . . . ? How to Achieve Discipline With Dignity in the Classroom* (1992, 2007), not satisfying a student's basic needs will trigger problem behaviors. These basic needs include:

- Feeling and believing that I am capable and can be successful here

- Knowing that I am noticed and cared about

- Realizing that I have influence because others are interested in my opinions and actions

- Seeing that I can make a difference in the lives of others because they look to me as a source of knowledge and help
- Experiencing the relevance of school to my life or seeing how it might be relevant at some future time
- Having fun and being stimulated by school
- Being secure that I am in a physically, emotionally, and intellectually safe place

When we use our understanding of these basic needs to guide our instructional strategies and interactive moments, fewer discipline problems occur because students want to behave.

Can you think of specific things that you are currently doing through the curriculum or in your interaction with students that are designed to address each of these basic needs? When you were a student, were there teachers or administrators who really seemed able to connect with all kinds of students? Are there any teachers or administrators like this at your school? What do they do?

INTERVENTION

Intervention is what we do when misbehavior occurs. The four goals of an effective intervention are outlined below.

Stop Misbehavior

This is the most obvious goal. Instruction is interrupted when a student says or does something offensive and inappropriate. The aim of all good discipline methods is to stop the misbehavior quickly.

Maintain Leadership

It is important to portray yourself as capable of dealing with inappropriate behavior. For us to remain effective and worthy of respect, our students need to believe we can effectively handle difficult situations in the same ways we want them to behave when faced with similar circumstances. For example, if I kick a student out of class for using an offensive gesture, then I have not taught my students anything useful for them to do should that same gesture be used to provoke them. Being a leader means presenting ourselves and handling the situation in a way that causes others to feel secure in our presence during difficult times.

Preserve Dignity

This is often the hardest goal to achieve because it is quite natural to have a "knee-jerk" reaction when our buttons are pushed. We must fight the impulse to strike back emotionally for three reasons:

1. We should use moments of conflict to model how we want our students to react when their buttons are pushed.

2. The misbehavior and knee-jerk responses will escalate because neither the teacher nor the student wants to appear weak in front of the other students. It is usually easier to end a power struggle when neither side feels that they have lost or been defeated.

3. Methods that preserve dignity are usually much more effective in the short term and long term. Destroying someone's dignity may force immediate compliance, but it virtually always builds resentment that will eventually lead to further escalation.

Recapture the Instructional Moment Quickly

It is vitally important to keep focused on recapturing the instructional moment as quickly as possible after a disruption has occurred. Otherwise, minor irritating moments can dominate the classroom climate and can have the undesirable effect of contagion. This is especially true with groups of challenging students. Keep in mind that most conflict is not going to be adequately resolved in the presence of an audience. The lion's share of effective long-term discipline occurs in the processing of the incident when adequate time is available to explore the confrontation with the student(s) involved. Effective intervention strategies essentially buy us time so we can return to instruction and postpone further exploration and discussion of the disruption with the student to a more appropriate time and place. For example, you are likely to more fully understand and resolve problems with an arguing student after class, when neither you nor the student feels compelled to "play" to the audience.

Some educators have difficulty knowing what to do when misbehavior happens, while others have a hard time maintaining self-control. Both knowing what to do and staying in control of oneself are necessary to being most effective during particularly challenging moments. What is most difficult for you when students are misbehaving?

SIX KEY CRITERIA TO CONSIDER WHEN CHOOSING A DISCIPLINE METHOD

Too often, discipline is a knee-jerk response that comes from frustration, anger, and the desire for retribution. There are six key questions educators need to ask when determining the effectiveness of a good discipline method:

1. What outcome do I want to achieve?
2. Is anyone getting better results?
3. Is the method working?
4. Does the method dignify or humiliate?
5. Is the method based on obedience, or does it teach responsibility?
6. How does the method affect the student's motivation to learn?

These criteria provide all the guidance needed to determine what to do with our students in order to facilitate better behavior.

1. What Outcome Do I Want to Achieve?

It is very important to begin with the end in mind. What is it you really want to accomplish? Be especially clear about what you are trying to do. Do you want the student to behave today during the test, come to class on time, or sit for a longer period of time during class than she has during the last 3 weeks? Be as specific as possible. It is common for difficult students to do a variety of things that we may find irritating. It will probably be easier to get a student to take his feet off a chair than it will be to have the student show a positive attitude throughout class. As Covey (1989) advises, "Begin with the end in mind."

2. Is Anyone Getting Better Results?

If you want to be successful at something, it is usually prudent to find people who have already attained the success you desire and examine what they did to get the results you seek. Are there teachers who have had or now have a troubling student in class and are achieving good, or better, behavior than you are achieving? Does this student have a favorite class or teacher? Can you free up some time to observe this teacher's style so that you can see what techniques might work for you?

I have worked with many "alternative" education teachers and students during my career. Many alternative programs have a primary goal of getting the student to perform and behave sufficiently well in the curriculum to warrant return to the "regular" program. Sadly, most students who earn their way back into the regular program fail to achieve success there. Inflexibility within the regular program is a major contributing factor to this lack of transfer of success from one program to the next. Too often success depends on the alternative student adjusting to the demands of the regular program. While this is a viable goal, it is interesting that the regular education staff virtually never reaches out to the alternative education staff to find out what was done to achieve success. Instead of attempting to adjust behavior and environment to replicate the success experienced elsewhere, many educators keep doing the same old things and then become angry or frustrated when kids fail to improve. Chances for behavioral success dramatically improve when we keep in mind the behavior we desire to achieve, look around to see what techniques have been successful, and are not afraid to mimic or apply those successful methods with our students.

3. Is the Method Working?

The most practical consideration is to ask yourself if your method is working. Clearly, an effective discipline method should lead toward better or improved behavior and less undesirable behavior. Once you develop a plan for improving behavior, implement it at least five times or for a trial period of 3 weeks. During this time, you should begin to see some evidence that better behavior is increasing, although the student may occasionally continue the undesirable behavior. Almost all change includes backsliding; as students improve their behavior, expect to see periodic returns to the old behavior. Change is a roller-coaster ride of ups and downs. When we see this roller-coaster pattern, we have evidence that the method is working, and that it is wise to continue using it. However, if there is little or no evidence of behavioral improvement during this period, be flexible and move on to another strategy. For example, if detention results in more evidence of better behavior lasting for a longer interval, continue to use detention with that student. If there is no indication of positive change, it is wise to try something else.

4. Does the Method Dignify or Humiliate?

Whether or not a method works is insufficient in deciding if it should be continued. For example, a severe threat from you to the student may achieve immediate results due to the fear the student instantly feels, but this quick result may lead to payback later. Therefore, it is equally important for us to assess how we might feel and be affected if we were on the receiving end of our method. For example, if we believe that a consequence would attack our dignity, we should consider something else. Ask yourself, "If somebody did this to me while trying to get me to behave according to his or her standards, would I feel his or her actions were an attack on my self-esteem, or would I leave with my dignity intact?" Think of all students as having tenure in your classroom, and treat them accordingly. When they misbehave, realize that your response needs to both stop the problem *and* keep the students motivated to learn. How we affect their dignity is perhaps the factor over which we have the greatest control in determining whether or not the problem continues.

5. Is the Method Based on Obedience, or Does It Teach Responsibility?

We need to consider whether or not the method teaches responsibility or merely elicits compliance. Although compliance is better than chaos, it is not as good as responsibility. Virtually all methods of behavior modification are about obedience, since we control all of the rewards and punishments. In the hands of caring educators, behavior modification methods can be very helpful in motivating students to change quickly. Most people will alter their behavior quickly if they know what is expected, have the ability to do what is expected, and value a promised reward for making the change. Unfortunately, these changes do not last unless they are eventually "owned" by the person for whom they are designed. In fact, it is common for students to behave in order to earn that first reward, but they will eventually resent the approach because they feel they are being controlled. Proper behavior is a worthy goal of all discipline methods, but the bigger job is to help students make choices and learn from the consequences of the choices they make. Responsibility is achieved by implementing methods of discipline that offer limits with choices. Good long-term discipline that teaches responsibility focuses on getting students to do the right thing because it is the right thing to do. Therefore, methods of behavior modification can be used to change behavior fast, but in order to make these changes last, methods that teach responsibility are necessary. Our work is not done if students comply in our presence but misbehave in our absence.

6. How Does the Method Affect the Student's Motivation to Learn?

When a discipline method is implemented at school, it is important that the technique positively affect student motivation. A method that controls behavior but turns students off to learning is harmful. For example, a suspended student who is overloaded with worksheets to be kept busy is likely to hate learning even more than he did before the suspension.

The best learning occurs when students are aroused and awakened to ask questions and challenge themselves, their teachers, and each other. If a discipline method gets a student to behave but scares her away from asking questions because she thinks humiliation will be the result if a mistake is made, then what might be viewed as an effective method of behavior control is, in fact, destructive to the very learning process we must encourage. When exploring a method of discipline, ask how the method might affect your desire to learn. Search for, observe, and learn from fellow educators who seem to promote good discipline while keeping students motivated to learn.

Part 2

Tips for Prevention

2 Tips for Welcoming Students

I passed Mr. Waxman in the hall. I had him last year for English, and even though I said hi to him, he walked right past me as if he never met me before.

—Lucas, age 16

Mrs. Hodges is really cool. Even though I only have her for one class period a day, I feel like I can talk to her about anything!

—Myeka, age 14

SET UP YOUR CLASSROOM IN A WELCOMING WAY

A new school year typically begins for teachers at least a few days before students arrive. The main purpose of this time is for organization of the classroom, although there is often some time set aside for professional development. A motivational speaker is often brought in to help inspire the "troops" on one educational theme or another. I have often been the motivational speaker for such groups, and I have usually been asked to address how to interact most effectively with students with difficult behavior. I am a veteran presenter and have learned to deal with just about every possible glitch in a calm and friendly manner, despite often remaining silently aghast at the surroundings in which I meet with my audience. Even though there has been an increased emphasis on the importance of environmental conditions to the success of a staff development day, it is not uncommon to encounter extremely difficult surroundings. For example, one may experience large numbers of teachers meeting in a poorly ventilated area (the cafeteria), seated tightly together on hard seats with a sound system that either echoes excessively or is barely audible. There may be the last-minute addition of an overhead projector that can barely be seen because it is of poor quality or cannot possibly be viewed by everyone in such a large room. Common interruptions include cell phones ringing or the constant drone of the intercom paging one person or another. Despite the presence of a professional speaker and motivated learners, I sometimes leave these experiences wondering if any meaningful learning could have occurred in this environment plagued with problems.

Working conditions matter! Just as there are limits to the effectiveness of an inspirational speaker in promoting learning among adults when working conditions are poor, there will also be limits to learning responsible behavior by the degree to which students feel welcome. The classroom environment sends subliminal messages to students, telling them how important we think they are. Although the way we arrange our classrooms may vary to reflect our content area and style of teaching, certain characteristics are agreeable in most every educational environment. Most individuals want to hear and see adequately, and feel physically comfortable. When concentration is required, people prefer not to be distracted by unnecessary interruptions. They like to be greeted in a personal way and respected for their opinions. They like a clean, pleasant, well-lighted place that conveys a sense of friendliness.

As you set up your classroom, be guided by what you find welcoming. For example, what makes you shop in certain stores? How do the employees treat you while you are in the store? Are they friendly, or do they ignore you? Does it depend, and what does it depend upon? What is the lighting like? Is there music in the background? Are the walls plain or decorated? What is the quality of the merchandise? Are you allowed to handle things, or are you even encouraged to handle things? Do you have to wait very long for assistance or is the service accommodating?

How do the characteristics above relate to your classroom? Which aspects do you believe you can arrange that would be conducive to the learning that needs to go on in the classroom? Most people learn best when they like being where they are.

LET "TLC" BE YOUR GUIDE

The usual definition of TLC has been adapted by Kindlon (2003) to mean *time, limits,* and *caring.* Although Kindlon provides this advice to parents, the same applies to educators: To be successful with your students, be guided by these three basics of TLC. The *time* element is very difficult during an era in which we are too often expected to be everything to everyone. The mantra of our time is to meet disparate student needs while making sure that they all achieve high standards. While time is at a premium, it is the greatest gift that we can offer our students. The gift is an extra moment to say hello, offer a high five, or provide help without being asked. The gift is taking that extra moment to recognize and acknowledge when a student seems troubled or to acknowledge when a troubling student has been behaving. A high-school teacher at a recent seminar shared her "2 × 180 strategy." She acknowledges each student for at least 2 seconds every day during the course of the 180-day school year (see page 33). *Limits* require that we establish a safe, predictable classroom structure complete with the routines and procedures associated with academic success. Limits are based on the values that are needed for learning to flourish. These include safety, respect, compassion, and responsibility. Finally, *caring* requires that we put a higher value on the students we teach than on the content they are expected to learn. Caring is best conveyed by noticing students on a regular basis. This can be as simple as saying, "I notice you have a red shirt on today." Each day, complete the following simple sentence with each of your students as they are arriving, departing, or during class: "*(Student's name),* I notice that you . . . "

A community sense of TLC develops when we help students look out for each other. Create opportunities for your students to serve others as helpers. Peer group tutoring and older students guiding younger students are a few simple ways to achieve this at school. Students who lack nurturing are actually nurtured while they foster others.

SHARING APPRECIATION

Appreciation Day. Getting students to appreciate each other is a good way to prevent discipline problems. There are many ways to do this. You could place a picture of each of your students along with his or her name on a large sheet of newsprint. Explain that each day one student's picture will be selected to hang on the bulletin board. Tell them that during certain times of the day (less structured times are best to minimize distractions), any student may go to the poster and write a statement that begins "One thing I like about you is . . . " Students could also draw pictures expressing their caring or appreciation of this student. No put-downs are allowed. Before the end of the school day, take a few minutes to permit students to file past the poster, and encourage them to read each statement or describe a drawing that they made on this poster. When finished, ask if there are any further expressions of appreciation. When the process is completed, put the child's poster away until his turn comes up again. After two rounds, allow each student the option of taking the poster home or displaying it in school.

The nice things list. With older students, do something similar to an activity first written about by a teacher, Helen Mrosla (Canfield & Hansen, 1993) in *Chicken Soup for the Soul*. Ask students to list the names of the other students in the class on two sheets of paper, leaving a space between each name. Tell them to think of the nicest thing they could say about each of their classmates and write it down. Collect all papers, and on a separate sheet of paper list each student's name followed by the things that everyone wrote about that individual. Then give students their papers to keep as a reminder that they are appreciated.

Kindness pail. Sally Levine, a first-grade teacher in Des Moines, Iowa, encourages students to observe little moments of kindness done by each other and to write or draw about these moments on a piece of paper. She then asks children to put their written "kindnesses" in a pail; every day before school ends, she reads a few of them. Ms. Levine noted that it seemed that some of her children would often receive many notes while others received very few. She suggests that it works well to encourage the children who receive many kind comments to share kind remarks about children who receive very few. She might say to them, "It is so wonderful that so many nice things are written about you, and all of them are true. You must feel very special hearing all those nice things. As the kind person that you are, I am going to ask you to do one more kindness. I am noticing that since _____ *(give names of children who get very few)* don't get very many kindness comments, it would help them feel special if you could think of something kind to write or draw about _____. Can I count on you to be especially kind in that way?"

Kindness link. A middle-school teacher attending one of my seminars told how her school encourages students to write down (on strips of colored paper) acts of kindness that they have seen or experienced. The hallway and cafeteria are decorated with these strips, which are linked together to form a chain.

"RB" time (relationship building). Make it easier on yourself and invest time for relationship-building every day. What you say or do does not have to be fancy—just saying hello to students as they enter the room, greeting them with a smile on your face, asking them how they are, or noticing something about how they look often tends to get the students "on your side." Offer a pat on the back and an encouraging "you can do it." When you show your students you are as concerned with who they are as with how well they do, it becomes much easier to gain their interest, respect, and compliance. Best of all, it only takes a few seconds to express something individual and personal that may become an enduring and positive memory for them.

You might think of a complimentary nickname for each student (make sure students clearly understand the significance). You could take a little time to send home an occasional postcard to each student specifically complimenting something about his or her effort or achievement. Bringing in cookies or another treat for a birthday is another way to show students how much you appreciate them. If you want to get a little more elaborate, you could select a "mystery" student of the week. Put each student's name on separate slips of paper in a container. Draw one student's name and place it in a sealed envelope. At the end of the week, open the envelope and identify the student. If the student has completed all assignments, the class earns a reward. The best strategy for protecting each student's dignity is to privately show the student that his or her name was drawn. If the student's behavior earned a reward, then the student has the option of having that fact announced to the class. If the behavior did not earn a reward, the feedback is given only to the student without anybody else knowing who it was. Building relationships improves student behavior and motivation.

The positive postcard. Periodically send home postcards addressed either to students or their parents that briefly outline and praise specific positive behavior or achievement you have recently observed. In doing this, the student will not only feel proud from the praise received from the teacher, but may also receive good words and encouragement at home.

Dear _____,

I just want to let you know how pleased I am with the effort you are showing in our class.

Thanks,

_____

The "2 × 180 strategy." As mentioned previously, another excellent strategy is for 2 seconds every day for 180 days (the entire school year or more if there are more days), endeavor to have a positive moment with each of your students. It can be as simple as smiling, saying hello, or commenting on something specific, such as, "I really like the effort you put into your paper."

Big Ziggy. For many years, I have been teaching the "H or H" strategy to teachers as a welcoming method. Every day, the teacher greets the children with a hug or a handshake. Over the years, this has been modified by others to include a *handshake, hello,* and *how are you?* For educators who are uneasy about giving a hug, you can instead use a stuffed animal. A teacher at one of my seminars named her animal "Big Ziggy." When you sense a child needing a hug (or as part of your daily greeting practice), you can put a stuffed animal between yourself and the child, hugging the child with the stuffed animal. This strategy has been found to work through at least the sixth grade.

CLASSROOM LEGACY

Brian Mendler, a special-education teacher and my son, shares an outstanding way of building relationships between students for the long-term success of your class. Have your class do a legacy project at the beginning of the school year (it can be done later on as well). Ask students to pick a topic that pertains to something they enjoy doing outside of school or that in a special way defines them. Be prepared for an extremely broad range of topics, and be sure to check the topics to make sure each is appropriate for a school presentation. At a secondary level, you can assign each student a 15- to 20-minute block of time to give an oral or written presentation to the class on that topic. With younger students, 5 to 10 minutes is adequate. It is advised that directions for the presentation be open-ended to encourage students to be creative. Students should try their best to include the rest of the class in their presentations. The goal is for students to get to know each other on a personal level. It also gives each individual a chance to be recognized for a special talent or interest.

The legacy project builds classroom community by giving students who do not normally communicate a chance to share. One autistic student named Mike shared his gift for art with the students in his English class. For his project, Mike brought many different paintings and drawings that he had completed. Although he was very nervous about speaking in front of the class, Mike gained tremendous confidence when he talked about his familiar topic. He demonstrated how to mix different paint colors and even gave each class member a chance to paint his or her own picture. His project was outstanding and gave other students a chance to know him on a different level. Mike went from being a student who was picked last and ignored, a student who often felt like an outcast, to being a highly valued member of the class. Another student who did this project was a swimmer who arranged to have the class come to the pool for her legacy presentation. The class watched as she swam the entire pool underwater and showed different synchronized swimming moves. Nobody in the class had known that she was such an excellent swimmer. Brian Mendler observes that by learning so much about his students' interests and talents early in the school year, he is often better able to adapt his curriculum to include projects and discussions in ways that more meaningfully involve them.

THE URGENT MESSENGER

Identify some of your students who are frequently disruptive. Approximately once every 2 weeks, ask each of them to deliver an important message—or what appears to the student to be an important message—to someone in the building (do this exercise more frequently for some if possible). For example, say to the student, "Betty, I have something in this envelope that has to get to Mr. Jones right away. You've got to make sure you get it there for me: Otherwise, there will be a big problem. Please go straight to Mr. Jones's classroom and come straight back so that this gets done."

Inside the envelope you can put in a blank sheet of paper or any message to the recipient—it really does not matter what message the envelope contains because this system will have been worked out ahead of time with a few faculty members who understand the purpose of this exercise. Use this strategy with students who require attention or want to feel special but seek recognition in the wrong way. You can use this procedure at your convenience, but it is best done when you begin to sense that this student may soon misbehave. In addition to making the student feel special, you also give him or her an opportunity for physical movement. This can help an uptight student "walk off" the frustration. Consider occasionally sending the messenger to a school administrator such as the assistant principal or principal. This will help the challenging student connect in a different way with a person who often plays the role of disciplinarian.

INVITE CHALLENGING STUDENTS TO PARTICIPATE IN EXTRACURRICULAR ACTIVITIES

Most students who have discipline problems feel cut off and out of place from the school's mainstream population. Some students who misbehave have difficulty learning. Although most schools have many organizations and clubs, few students with discipline problems actively seek involvement in extracurricular school events and activities. Welcoming and encouraging these students to join school organizations, clubs, and activities can prevent problems from occurring or continuing. Try to learn about the interests of these students. Talk to them in an effort to determine their in-school or out-of-school interests, and be the person who helps them become more connected. You might also develop an interest inventory or use the reproducible inventory on the next two pages to learn about students' preferences.

My Interest Inventory

Name _____

Please complete the following sentences:

- Something I like to do out of school is_____
  _____.

- My favorite time of year is _____
  _____.

- People I respect are_____
  _____.

- When I was younger, I used to _____
  _____.

- When I get older, I hope to _____
  _____.

- I wish _____
  _____.

- During my free time, I prefer_____
  _____.

- A place I would like to visit is_____
  _____.

- I feel most needed when _____
  _____.

- At school _____
  _____.

- When I am alone _____
  _____.

- With other people _____
  _____.

- My favorite sport is _____
  _____.

- My favorite music is _____
  _____.

- I would really like it if somebody at school asked me to
  _____.

- It would be helpful for my parent/guardian to _____
  _____.

- My favorite subject in school is _____
  _____.

- Some interests I wish my teachers would focus more on
  would be _____
  _____.

- I like to learn new things by _____
  _____
  (seeing, listening, doing, and so on).

- Not too many people know that _____
  _____.

FIFTEEN QUICK AND ENCOURAGING STATEMENTS

Words of encouragement can keep kids connected and motivated. Below are 15 sentences that take little time to say. Just think of the influence you can have if you share one of these statements each day with 15 different students.

Encouraging Statements for Students

1. Way to go!

2. How thoughtful.

3. Wow—outstanding.

4. That was awesome.

5. You really hung in there.

6. You brighten my day.

7. Look at the smile you have put on my face.

8. I hope you feel proud because you should.

9. That was quite an accomplishment.

10. Congratulations.

11. I was so impressed today when _____.

12. This is really challenging stuff we did today, and you stayed with it.

13. I am one lucky teacher to have a class (or student) who _____ when _____.

14. The progress I saw today when you did _____ was impressive.

15. That took a special effort.

ACCENTUATE THE POSITIVE CONCERNING NEGATIVE BEHAVIOR

As unusual as this might sound, challenging students are much more apt to cooperate and comply when we find a way to appreciate the very behavior, or elements within that behavior, we would like to change. Start by telling the student what is good about the behavior. For example, a student who is often out of his seat can be viewed as energetic and enthusiastic. You might say, "Joey, you are a very energetic person and full of life, so I know how hard it is for you to stay in your seat. I bet you love to move and run. Is that right?"

The next step is to explain to the student how the behavior creates a problem for you, and for other students. For example, explain: "Joey, here is my problem. When you move around during work time, it is hard for some of the other children who need peace and quiet to do their work." Follow by asking for the child's help, making a deal, and thanking the child for his cooperation: "I really need your help, Joey. How about staying in your seat until Jack finishes his work? Then you can get up and take a walk around the room. Does that sound good to you? Thanks for your help."

In review, the specific steps are:

1. Tell the student what is good about the behavior that you want to see changed:

   "Amy, you are one of the most . . . *(identify the problem as if it is a strength)* I know."

2. Briefly explain how the behavior creates a problem either for you or for other students:

   "But my problem is that when you . . . *(name or describe the specific behavior)*, it makes it difficult for me to . . . *(explain to the student the difficulties posed by his or her behavior)*."

3. Make a specific request by asking for the child's help in solving the problem:

   "So do you think you could . . . *(make a request by telling the student what you want)*."

4. Offer an incentive or a trade-off for the child's cooperation, showing your willingness to meet the child's needs:

   "And then maybe after we're finished, you could . . . *(offer an incentive or propose a trade-off)*."

5. Thank the child for the substantial effort it is likely to take for success to occur.

   "Amy, thank you so much for your super effort today. I really appreciate all your help. . . ." *(Thank the student before compliance occurs. This increases the chances that the student will do as you ask.)*

3 Tips for Developing Effective Rules and Consequences

I love my school. Not all the teachers are interesting, but they care. And the kids are nice, too. Even though there are cliques, people respect each other. Nobody is allowed to bully. My school feels safe.

—Lisa, age 13

TIPS FOR SCHOOL-WIDE DISCIPLINE

Every school has divergent opinions about discipline. At the extremes are the "bleeding hearts" who act as if all disruptive students are victims and therefore need more love and caring. Then there is the "hang them high" crowd who believe that a tough, punitive approach is the answer. Naturally, most educators are somewhere in between. Students need to realize there are individual differences between teachers—not all share the same ideas and will not, therefore, have the same rules and consequences. We have long advocated for student involvement in developing rules and consequences. Each teacher is advised to establish rules based upon the content/approach to be taught and his or her style. For example, a teacher of industrial technology may need rules about safety that would be unnecessary in an English class. While individual differences are encouraged, it is also necessary to make sure that all educators are in agreement. It is therefore advisable for each school to develop a set of principles, or values, that pertain to everyone who serves in that educational environment—teachers, administrators, and staff. These values will serve as the framework upon which all staff members convey their disciplinary rules so that we all send a consistent message. There are three primary principles that many schools have adopted to bind educators together:

1. Take care of yourself.

2. Take care of each other.

3. Take care of this place.

Based upon these three principles, each teacher is advised to develop a discipline plan with his or her students. The plan should include specific procedures, rules, and consequences that are necessary in order for good teaching and learning to occur. Students can actively engage in this process by suggesting rules that are compatible with each principle. Finally, school-wide discipline requires some compromise and sacrifice. For example, common areas such as the cafeteria and the halls need carefully outlined parameters (rules) so that order prevails. We must all enforce rules in these common areas *even if we disagree with them.* Not every teacher or administrator will have the same view of students who wear hats, for instance, but if there is a rule about hats, then all must enforce it. To do otherwise is to subtly undermine the system, and students will come to believe that the only rules they need to follow are those with which they agree. Work to change the rules if you disagree with them, but enforce them until they are changed.

Although rules and consequences are an important element in establishing an orderly, safe environment, the most critical factors that make for effective school-wide discipline are *effective leadership* and *active adult visibility*. The school leader must be a welcoming individual with a clear vision whose presence is felt by all. While the leader seeks and values input from all school groups, there is no ambiguity about who really is in charge. The leader is accountable to all and takes responsibility for his or her actions and decisions, including those that may be unpopular. Although compromise may at times be necessary, decisions are based primarily on what is educationally sound rather than on what may be politically correct. Teachers who are actively visible convey a feeling of supervision and safety to their students. Strive to be in the hallways, stairwells, and cafeteria in an engaged way, making eye contact with students. Briefly greeting them warmly can work wonders in securing cooperation when disciplinary action is needed. When unruly behavior has been the norm within the school or at a specific location, schools are wise to create zones of supervision in which staff members are assigned an area to patrol. It is advisable to have two adults near each other within a radius of approximately 150 feet so that support is available if it is needed.

SHOW PROPER WAYS FOR CHANGING RULES

It is wise to strictly keep and maintain rules that promote learning and safety, but to negotiate rules that may be preferred but are not necessary. No responsible educator would argue against the wisdom of having and enforcing rules pertaining to drugs and violence, but some are certain to think it folly to have rules about chewing gum. If there are school rules with which you disagree, work to get those changed. Try pointing out to those in charge how the rule makes it more difficult for you to teach or more difficult for your students to learn. When students complain about rules that students and staff consider to be stupid or poorly conceived, develop a strategy that might change the system. At an alternative high school where I consulted, interviews with students revealed considerable resentment about having locked bathrooms. Each time a student needed to use the restroom, an adult had to unlock the door. It turned out that locking the bathrooms was the staff's solution to controlling smoking, loitering, and littering. The staff was just as displeased with playing cop as the students were in having their freedom curtailed. I suggested that the student council be presented with the option of having the bathrooms unlocked if they could come up with an alternative that would address the issues of smoking, loitering, and littering. Following several rounds of discussions between student council and staff representatives, a plan was developed that included joint staff and student monitoring of the bathrooms, along with specific directives concerning how the bathrooms would be cleaned by the students if littering persisted.

If you need to enforce a rule with which you disagree, try appealing more to your relationship with the student rather than the sensibility of the rule. For example, say, "Steve, I know you think it is stupid to have to take off your hat. But if you don't, I'm stuck between a rock and a hard place. I have to write up a referral, which wastes your time and mine. Thanks for your cooperation." If the student resists, enforce the consequence but collaborate later with the student to explore ways of changing the rule—such as arranging for a meeting with the principal or signing up the student to voice his or her opinion at a school board meeting.

INVOLVE STUDENTS IN MAKING AND MODIFYING CLASSROOM RULES

Students are more likely to follow, monitor, and enforce rules when they have ownership of them. There are several good ways to involve students in the rule-making process without sacrificing leadership.

Identify Class Principles or Values and Ask Students to Create Rules

First outline and discuss with your students the values necessary for good teaching and learning to occur. These can include specifics such as, "We expect a safe learning environment," and "We are to use the language and attitude of respect toward each other, especially when we disagree with someone else."

Students are then expected to come up with specific rules to be followed that are compatible with these values. The rules students propose are virtually identical to the same ones they hear from us, such as, "Use words, not fists," and "Don't take stuff without obtaining permission."

Invite Students to Develop Rules for the Teacher

The teacher may ask students to propose rules that they believe will help them learn more effectively. For example, students propose a rule that requires papers and tests to be handed back within 3 days. This can assist learning and is therefore reasonable. Agreeing to give choices in topics for a required essay or test questions on a test also seems quite reasonable. By contrast, a rule stating "no homework ever" would not be acceptable since homework is designed to support and reinforce learning.

Ask Students to Develop Rules for Each Other

You can allow the students to develop rules (and possibly consequences) for each other. As noted above, all rules proposed by students must be compatible with classroom values. Do not accept any rule or consequence that you will not feel comfortable enforcing.

Define the Rules and Consequences, but Then Invite Students to Share Their Opinions for Possible Changes

This method requires the teacher to specify the rules and then solicit suggestions for changes from the students. For example, the teacher might say to the students, "In past years I have found that most students like to know that no one will be allowed to take their stuff without permission. How many of you think this would be a good rule for our class?" Another example would be, "Some third grade teachers think that students should miss recess if they don't do their work. We're going to do that also, unless somebody has a better idea."

It is quite possible to use some variation of our system of government in establishing classroom values and rules. Miles Watts' third-grade class at Sherman School in Rochester, New York, used the U.S. Constitution as a model for developing classroom rules (see pages 50 and 51). By involving students in the development of rules, we teach them the values and foundations upon which our way of life is based: democracy, involvement, responsibility, and compromise. Just as our system of government has checks and balances, be sure to review your classroom rules and consequences regularly. Fine-tuning is needed periodically, so be sure to review the rules and consequences every few weeks. Celebrate when things are going well, and work with your students to modify the rules if things are not progressing adequately.

REVIEW RULES REGULARLY AND CONSIDER EMPHASIZING A "RULE OF THE WEEK"

Most teachers establish rules and consequences during the first few days of school. Although it is wise to let students know what is expected early, many students grimace with boredom at the mention of the word "rules." After all, they have heard this word numerous times since kindergarten, and since all teachers have similar rules, it is not uncommon for students to tune out. They think they have heard it all before. Therefore, rules should be reviewed soon after classes begin and then again on a monthly basis. In this way, students can hear favorable remarks about the rules they have followed and be encouraged to improve those that are being broken. Helpful ideas can be solicited from students in your classes. For example, tell your students, "We have done very well at showing respect by listening while others are talking. Things haven't gone quite as well with all of us remembering to stay seated during the class. Who has ideas about how we can help those who have a harder time remaining seated during class?"

Another way to keep rules fresh and meaningful is to consider highlighting one or two rules during a specific interval of time— making it a kind of "rule du jour" but for a weekly or semiweekly period of time. Emphasize these rules, and lead thorough discussions regarding them. Post them, but resist the temptation to cover the classroom walls with all of the rules you have discussed because this tends to be overwhelming. Students should clearly understand they are expected to follow rules, but the highlighted rules should be presented as a special challenge. For example, you might say, "Since lining up is still difficult, let's make a special effort this week to concentrate on following that rule."

CHARACTERISTICS OF EFFECTIVE CONSEQUENCES

Many educators are continuously on the lookout for effective consequences for difficult students. Appropriate and effective disciplinary tools can be tough to find. Some students are quite resistant and act as if they took consequences immunization shots before they entered the classroom. It is a mistake, therefore, to rely heavily upon rules and consequences for effective discipline. Many schools have thick handbooks with a thousand rules that most students will never become aware of because they are already sufficiently well-behaved. At the same time, students who are chronically in trouble are rarely deterred by the rules and consequences. So while it is naïve to believe that consequences alone can control behavior, consequences can be effective tools for improvement when done properly.

There are many possible kinds of consequences, but those that are natural or logical are most likely to improve behavior. A consequence should be designed to teach better behavior. It should not primarily focus on misery, although if learning accompanies the misery, then it is okay. Examples of natural and logical consequences

The Classroom Constitution
2002–2003

We the people of room B-13, in order to make our classroom a better place to be, establish justice, ensure peace in school and out, stick up for one another, promote fun education, and secure these ideas for this school year, do hereby declare this Classroom Constitution.

Article I—The Students

Section 1. All students shall make every effort to be nice, patient for the teacher's help, respectful, kind to others, polite, safe, cool, fun, sympathetic, helpful, peaceful, encouraging, caring, and honorable.

Section 2. All students shall make every effort to treat others the way they want to be treated, say "good morning" every day, help each other if needed, not argue, let other classmates join their activities, accept others for who they are, give everyone a chance to talk in the group, think before speaking, use appropriate language, work together, not be pathetic, pay attention to others, and have a good attitude.

Section 3. No student shall tease, or make fun of, another student in a hurtful way.

Section 4. All students must tell Mr. Watts when they need to leave the classroom.

Article II—The Teacher

Section 1. Mr. Watts shall make every effort to be groovy, cool, kind, caring, friendly, fun, nice, peaceful, thankful, sympathetic, helpful, honest, encouraging, responsible, and safe.

𝔖ection 2. Mr. Watts should also make every effort to have a sense of humor, make learning fun, care for all students, give students time to ask questions, give kids chances, play guitar often, have fun with every subject, teach in creative ways, give students responsibility, play kickball and fly the kite, give students free time, go on field trips with the class, and use learning games.

𝔖ection 3. Mr. Watts may not, at any time, yell at the class or an individual.

𝔖ection 4. Mr. Watts will allow students an opportunity to complete report cards of him and the classroom in order to learn and improve his teaching.

𝔄rticle 𝔍𝔍𝔍—𝔒ur 𝔆lassroom

𝔖ection 1. We all will strive to do our best and learn from our mistakes.

𝔄rticle 𝔍𝔙

𝔖ection 1. This constitution may be amended or changed.

Mr. Watts	Kristen	BETSY	CAITLYN
Adam	Richard	Steven	Nicole
Karan	Chelsea	Stacy	Chris
Sierra	Anna	Carliss	COREY
Jesse	Jessica	Maddie	Tom
Stephie	Aaron		

include staying after school to complete an overdue assignment, cleaning up the mess after a food fight, repairing defaced school property, working off the debt incurred by damaging school or personal property, and making restitution by helping someone after they have been hurt. There must be a clear connection made between the rule that was broken and what happens as a result of breaking the rule.

A consequence must teach better behavior. Just as each student is special and individual, a consequence must be individually *flexible* while simultaneously *predictable* in order for maximum results from the application of the consequence to be achieved and learned. Consequences should never be viewed as "one size fits all." In order to remain predictable and flexible, let your students know that if they break rules in your presence, there will be consequences. When deciding on the application of a consequence as a result of misbehavior, two primary things must be considered: *intent,* what was meant, and *impact,* what was done. Let your students know you will do whatever it takes to help someone learn better behavior, and let them know that you will sometimes apply different consequences among students—just as you will sometimes ask students to read from different books. To maintain effectiveness concerning the consequences delivered, it is advised that instead of sequencing the consequences in a "1-2-3-4-5" manner (also known as the "ladder" approach, in which the consequence is given based upon how many times the rule is broken), set up consequences as "A-B-C-D-E." Let your students know that if rules are broken, one or more of the consequences will be given based upon what you believe will best teach the student better behavior. Finally, if a student protests the consequence, be open to having the student select another alternative that will help that student learn better behavior. Then hold the student accountable!

Traits of Effective Consequences

- Effective consequences must be clear, specific, and easy to understand.

- Effective consequences provide a wide range of alternatives for matching the consequence to the particular student and circumstance in a way that best instructs the student about good behavior.

- Effective consequences are designed primarily to teach rather than to create misery or unhappiness.

- As closely as possible, the effective consequence needs to relate to the rule not being followed.

- Effective consequences must preserve the student's dignity.

- Effective consequences do not harm one's motivation to learn.

CONSIDER USING STUDENTS TO CREATE CONSEQUENCES

Involving your students in the creation and selection of consequences can heighten their participation, ownership, and responsibility. It generally works best to tell them which consequences you usually find effective, while inviting them to propose any other suggestions for consequences that they believe might work better. Let them know that a consequence should teach better behavior, and ask them to share a consequence they have experienced that achieved results. Students can actually be much harsher towards each other when identifying consequences, so be careful to keep the focus on *teaching* better behavior rather than on creating as much *misery* as possible. Most educators can comfortably tell students, "The following consequences are what I have found works best with most students to help them learn after a rule is broken. Can anyone think of other consequences we can add to make our rules work even better?"

When it comes to implementing consequences, it is best to be a little flexible. For example, say, "Joe, you know that hands and feet need to be kept to yourself. What consequence(s) do you think will best help you not make the same mistake again?"

If your students are not responding to consequences, you will need to revisit this issue with them: "Even though we have a rule to use respectful language, the consequences are not making the situation better. What else do you think we might do to solve this problem?" Some teachers contend that they prefer to sequence or "ladder" their consequences. While this is generally not advisable since it often locks educators into implementing a consequence without regard to whether it is likely to be effective (see "Characteristics of Effective Consequences" on page 49), the structure provided by the "ladder" method makes some educators feel secure. It is desirable under these situations to let students know that the "ladder" is in effect and will be implemented if rules are broken. However, students should be advised that if they ever think something else will work better than the laddered consequence, they are welcome to share their idea with you.

Finally, it is even possible to introduce an element of humor and suspense with consequences. A middle-school English teacher made singing a song a consequence for coming late to class. She indicated that since implementing this consequence, students arrive promptly to avoid having to sing for everyone. Bob Lewis, a high-school teacher, developed a "Wheel of Misfortune," which is patterned after the popular television show. If students break rules, they either accept the consequence(s), choose one or more consequence(s) they believe will work better, or are given the option of spinning the Wheel of Misfortune. Each spoke of the wheel has a different consequence. After a rule has been broken, Bob often simply says with a hint of humor to the student, "You know that was against the rules, so either stop or spin."

Wheel of Misfortune

EASY MATH: FAIRNESS = SUCCESS + RESPONSIBILITY

Many educators are frustrated with students and their parents who endlessly complain about unfair treatment. To be successful in discipline, you must do what is effective with each student without worrying about accusations from other students and their parents that you are unfair. Make a distinction between being "fair" and "treating everyone the same." Students and their parents should be assured that as educators we do all that we can to treat students fairly when "fair" is properly defined. Students and parents need to sincerely know that we will do our best to give students what they need in order to be *successful* in their studies and in their lives, and to help in whatever ways we can for them to learn to be *responsible.*

Given the intellectual, academic, and behavioral diversity present in most classrooms, instruction is virtually always based upon the premise that as educators we strive to be fair, but fairness is based upon individuality. It is common for teachers to be using multiple curricula simultaneously in their differentiated classrooms. Just as you individualize academically, do so behaviorally. Let your students and their parents know that if rules are broken, you will do whatever is necessary to help them not break the same rule again. Tell them that you have only two goals that guide your teaching for all children: *successful learning* and the learning of *responsibility*.

Apply this to all aspects of your teaching. Stay open to the prospect of an alternative working better, but make sure that if an alternative consequence or intervention is suggested, the person making the suggestion is clear about how success and responsibility will be better achieved. So if Myra complains because both she and Sarah were "doing the same thing" and Sarah got off easy, you might say, "Myra, if you are saying that you want the same consequence as Sarah, are you also saying that you will immediately improve your behavior?" If the answer is "yes," my advice is to give her whatever consequence she wants. A consequence should be looked at as a vehicle that we use as we travel to our destination. Be flexible about the vehicle, but persistent and determined about the destination.

Consider expressing yourself in the following way if parents complain about unfair treatment that you have given their child:

> Thank you for caring enough about your child to express your concerns, and before I explain the reason(s) for my actions, I want to say that I think your child is extremely lucky to have parents who care as much as you do to disagree with what I did. There are two goals that I have for your child and every other student who enters my class. I want each to be *successful* in his or her education and life, and I want all to learn something more about *responsibility*

56

as it relates to learning. If you think there is a better way to help your child become either more successful or more responsible in this class, I hope you will share your thoughts with me. I will certainly respect your point of view. However, please don't ask that I even try to treat all of my students exactly the same way. I have many students in my class(es), and I do whatever it takes to reach every single one of them. My question is: Did I miss the boat with your child? What do you think might work better? Are there things that work at home, for instance, that help your child be successful and responsible there?

GIVE A TEST FOR COMPREHENSION OF THE PRINCIPLES, RULES, AND CONSEQUENCES

After rules and consequences have been established, give a test for comprehension. This will eliminate the "I didn't know" excuse phenomenon that is all too common among some students. With younger students, you can connect the earning and continuation of classroom privileges to achieving a 100% score. Older students can bank extra points for passing the test or earn them outright. It is wise to expect a perfect score at all levels, since the test covers the classroom policy defining appropriate behaviors and what they are based upon. Sample questions follow:

- Besides a notebook or folder, what else do you have to bring to class every day?

- What is the time limit for a lavatory pass?

- What consequences are likely to happen if you are late for class?

- If students have a problem with each other, how are they allowed to work things out?

- When students think they are being bullied or harassed, what are they supposed to do?

- If students hear a put-down directed towards somebody else, do they have any responsibility towards helping the person respond? What are some things to do?

- True or False—Getting out of your seat whenever you want is okay.

- What are three acceptable things you can do if you disagree with a teacher?

4 Tips for Promoting Greater Responsibility and Problem-Solving Abilities

The teachers at my school care about what we think. Students have lots of responsibilities, not just for themselves but for each other, also. The principal meets every few weeks with a group of students and asks for their opinions on things.

—Fred, age 12

FOCUS ON BUILDING THE FOUNDATIONS OF RESPONSIBILITY: AWARENESS, CHOICE, AND PLANNING

Students who handle responsibility poorly are nearly always lacking in one or more of the three main building blocks in teaching responsibility: *awareness, choice,* and *planning.* Some students simply do not reflect upon what they are doing before they act: impulsiveness characterizes their behaviors. Most mean no harm, but are so driven by their impulse that they do not stop and reflect before acting. These students lack *awareness.* Other students do not or cannot see the connection between the choices they make and the conse-quences of their actions. These students have problems with making good *choices*. Finally, some students present themselves in a disorganized, even chaotic way. Students who lack good *planning* skills are often very easily distracted and driven more by the events of the moment than they are by a comprehensive assessment of what is going on around them. As most educators know, many students who evidence little responsibility have gaps in more than one of these basic building blocks.

I teach a simple three-step process that educators can use with students to illustrate how these building blocks can work together. After performing an unacceptable behavior, a student may be instructed to complete the following sentences at his or her desk or in a time-out area either inside or outside of the classroom. This can be done with or without adult supervision, although it virtually always requires adult follow-up:

1. Today I had a problem with _____. *(awareness)*

2. The bad choice I made was _____. *(choice)*

3. Next time I will do better at _____. *(planning)*

The strategies in this section are designed to either build or further develop these three foundations of responsibility.

USE PROPS TO HELP PROMOTE RESPONSIBILITY

Some students act irresponsibly because they lack awareness of what they are doing even after they know the rules. Examples include chronic daily misconduct such as pencil tapping, talking out of turn, socializing, and getting out of their seats. When these behaviors have an automatic quality about them, students usually know what is right and wrong but lack awareness that they are actually participating in the behavior. It is not uncommon when confronted for such students to genuinely appear concerned and express an apology. Unfortunately, apologies rarely lead to sustained improvement. There are some techniques that can be of great assistance in promoting student awareness and in managing their behavior. Teachers can readily use a variety of sensory props and physical movement to obtain results.

Mouse pad. This is a good method to consider for students who noisily tap on their desks and seem to lack awareness. Give them each a mouse pad and ask them to pretend the mouse pad is a drum top. Tell them to tap away on the mouse pad instead of directly on their desks, so that they get the physical movement they desire while keeping things quiet. When you have a chorus of drummers who you think might benefit from the mouse technique, you can purchase a few pads and then cut each into quarters. In this way, one pad can effectively be used with as many as four students.

Laminated ear. Carole Lindley, a fifth-grade teacher in Minneapolis, made an 18-inch tall laminated ear and placed it in a corner of the classroom as a way of symbolically dealing with the issue of "tattling." After repeated attempts to explain the distinction between telling and tattling, Carole told the class, "Unfortunately, I don't always have the time to listen to each of you about everything you want to tell me. So  from now on, if you are bothered about what someone says or does, and their actions are not dangerous, destructive, or demeaning—tell the ear." Carole reports that some students use the ear for this purpose while others use the ear as a means of getting things off their chest when there is nobody immediately available to listen.

Signs or drawings. During a high school observation, I noticed a large sign hanging above a wastebasket in the classroom. The sign said, "Deposit all trash talk here." When I asked the teacher why the sign was there, she told me that put-downs and street language had been quite common among her students. The sign was a reminder that acceptable language in the classroom was required. To emphasize the importance of this reminder, she told me that each time a student used unacceptable language, she either pointed toward the sign or crumpled a piece of paper into a ball and tossed it into the wastebasket under the sign. She indicated that it is rarely necessary for her to do more than this when she hears inappropriate language.

Color-coded cards. Alan Merrill, a teacher at Briggs Middle School in Springfield, Oregon, laminates three cards of different colors to help deal with the issue of students shouting out answers that may or may not be related to the topic. Before students speak, they must hold up one of three cards: The green card means that what they are about to say is strongly related to the topic; yellow means that their words also have something to do with the topic but are not as pertinent; red means that what they are about to say does not deal with the topic of discussion at all (they might want to ask for a bathroom pass or a new pencil). Alan has found this to be extremely effective in making kids think about their responses (awareness) as well as improving overall communication skills among the students.

Ugly shoes. Mickey Tisdale, a sixth-grade social studies teacher in Indianapolis, Indiana, has a pair of sneakers with steel toes and orange shoestrings. When Mickey is having a bad day or a class has been very unruly, she will put these shoes on before the next class starts. Ms. Tisdale tells her kids at the beginning of the year that when they see her wearing her ugly shoes, they should take note and act as respectfully as they would toward their own mothers when "mom is having a bad day."

Colored paper clips. Barbara Klein, a special-education teacher in Rochester, New York, has a lot of different colored paper clips. Each color of paper clip represents an individual student, and Barb uses these as a monitoring system for individuals who have excessive behaviors, such as blurting out, being out of their seats, and using put-downs.

Each time a student does a targeted behavior, she puts that student's color of paper clip into a separate pocket. At the end of a predetermined interval (the period, morning, or day), she shows the student how many paper clips have been accumulated. The goal is for the students to receive the smallest number of paper clips possible. She then develops an appropriate behavior plan to help students reach that goal.

The 2-cent jar. A primary level special-education teacher invented this method. She begins each week by putting 2 dollars in pennies into a jar. Each time someone interferes with another student's business, she removes 2 cents from the jar. At the end of the week, the remaining money is divided in half, with part going to a charity that helps people and part being saved for an eventual classroom treat or reward.

Using music to build awareness. B. Mayberry of Garnet Valley Elementary School plays music to help students stay focused and not talk at inappropriate times. He has students select a popular song, and then he puts it on tape or burns it to a CD. Whenever students start to talk without permission, the music is played until the talking stops. At the end of the day, if there is still music remaining on the tape, the students get 5 to 10 minutes to talk with friends while the music plays in the background. If there is no music left, then there is no talking.

Using "proper" language. Jody Gordon, a high-school teacher at an alternative school in Henrico County, Virginia, refuses to accept offensive language. He humorously confronts his students when they swear and then requires them to use the proper term. For example, if a student says "bulls--t," he will immediately say, "No Bill, that would be 'bull feces.'" The all too familiar "f--- you" becomes "intercourse you." Mr. Gordon seizes control of these moments by dramatically exaggerating his inflection and body language as he offers the alternative.

ASK *WHAT,* NOT *WHY*

We are much more likely to stop misbehavior and simultaneously contribute to developing responsibility when we confront inappropriate behavior by asking students, "What are you doing?" rather than, "Why are you misbehaving?" *Why* questions make it easy for students to externalize their thinking. This is already prevalent among students who do not act in a responsible way. Here are a few typical responses given by difficult students to *why* questions about behavior: "He did it first," "Because I felt like it," "I wanted to," "I don't know," and "I wasn't doing anything." None of these answers reflects internalized thinking, which is a very important first step in acquiring responsibility. We must help students look inward, or else they are likely to blame others, events, or circumstances rather than taking responsibility for their behavior. A fairly common response from difficult students to a "what are you doing" question is the answer, "nothing." This stumps and frustrates many educators unnecessarily. An excellent response that usually stops the misbehavior and promotes responsibility is to ask, "What are you *supposed* to be doing?" It is usually most effective to conclude the sequence by saying, "Don't tell me now because this is not a good time for me to listen, but thank you for doing it right now. I appreciate it." It is wonderful to gain compliance from most difficult students while at the same time contributing to their development of responsibility.

To further build on the responsibility theme, you might post four questions to get or keep students focused:

1. What are you doing?
2. What are you supposed to be doing?
3. What should you do next?
4. What should you not be doing?

TEACH STUDENTS THE POWER OF PLANNING

In many instances, students in trouble believe that there is only one way to solve a problem. They do not realize that other choices are available. Many come from impulsive and unpredictable families. They are either uncertain about or lack access to any other ways of handling a difficult situation. When discussing a problem with a student, it can be very helpful to lead him or her through the following planning process. This sequence can be done orally or in writing:

- What did you do that got you into trouble?

- When you did that, what did you want to happen?

- What else could you have done? *(Ask the student to list at least three other possibilities.)*

- If you get into trouble again for doing this, what consequence(s) do you think would be fair for you?

- What will you do the next time you are faced with this situation?

Here is another effective planning process:

- What happened?

- Do you think this could ever happen again?

- When problems happen, there is usually more than one person to blame. Who else could you blame for the problem you are having?

- What did they do?

- What did you do?

- If you really do not want to get into trouble again, and someone does the same thing to bother you, what can you do next time to avoid getting into trouble?

KEEP A PROBLEM-SOLVING BOOK

Ms. Jones, a second-grade teacher in Chicago, Illinois, has a novel approach to helping her students solve their minor problems or concerns without being directly involved. When minor problems occur that could consume considerable teacher time, the children in conflict are given choices: Accept the teacher's consequences, solve their problems together in a relatively private classroom location, or use a mediator (a trained fellow student) to help them solve their problems. Most of the time one or more of these choices works well. However, when problem(s) are not solved or reappear, the students who are in conflict have to write about the problem(s) they are having in a classroom problem book. At the end of the week, Ms. Jones reads the written problems that have accumulated during the week to the entire class and then encourages her students to help by offering possible solutions. Sometimes the time frame for reading the problems to the class changes, especially when Ms. Jones believes that brainstorming with the class should be done immediately or if a student in conflict makes a request. If students wrote down a problem but then solved it after the mediation but before the class problem-solving meeting, they remove the problem from the book. Ms. Jones expends far less class time handling minor irritating behaviors because her students know that they are empowered to deal directly with each other, equipped with the skills for doing so, and are supported with back-up help through mediation or whole-class problem-solving when necessary.

THREE EASY STOP-AND-THINK LEARNING STRATEGIES: THINK ALOUD, PROBLEM-SOLVING, AND MILLIONAIRE

There are several short, focused techniques that can help children develop better self-control. The goal is to get a student to think before acting. Those students who have difficulty stopping and thinking before acting can accrue dramatic benefits by learning and practicing structured self-questioning methods.

Think aloud. In "Think Aloud," children are trained to ask themselves each of the following questions and then provide an answer before moving on to the next question:

1. What is my problem?

2. What is my plan to solve the problem?

3. Am I using my plan?

4. What should I do?

Problem-solving. There are additional questions that can be included in the process depending upon the child and his or her specific needs. For example, "Have I considered all of my choices?" and "What are the consequences of each choice?" *Cognitive Behavior Modification* (Meichenbaum, 1977) presents the following sequence:

1. What am I supposed to do?

2. I need to look at all of the possibilities.

3. I have to focus in and concentrate.

4. I have to make a choice.

5. How well did I do?

Some students who are especially poor at planning need to rehearse saying each step of an action before actually doing the action: "First I need to get my book bag and open it. Next I need to take out the red folder (color-coded for each subject) and a pencil. Then I need to turn to the page listed on the board and read the directions."

Does anyone want to be a millionaire? Finally, on the television show, *Who Wants to Be a Millionaire,* contestants are allowed three "lifelines" on their way to riches. When stumped by a question, they can poll the audience, ask an expert (people they had identified as potential helpers before the show), or request a 50/50 (the correct answer provided among two choices rather than four). These three options can be built into your classroom when any student has a problem. Let your students know that whenever they confront a problem, before they act they can first use their lifelines. They can:

- Poll (or ask) the class what they think a good solution might be.

- Ask an expert (someone they think is especially good at handling the problem).

- Use a 50/50. In this case, offer students two choices that are acceptable to you, and allow them to select the one they find more preferable.

You can reinforce this strategy by posting a description of these three options in a place that easily reminds your students about resources they can use when they face a tough problem.

EMPOWER AGGRESSIVE STUDENTS—BUT SET LIMITS

Aggressive behavior that is hurtful is usually the result of frustration caused by inner feelings of inadequacy. Too often, aggressive students have very little actual influence in their lives. Conflict with others gives them a sense of control, especially when they can become dominant. Even when they lose, the experience of feeling important enough to anger someone else outweighs the pain of losing or the rejection from peers. Naturally, limits need to be established and enforced around harmful expressions of aggressive behavior. Conventional consequences can include time-out, developing a plan, and detention. Positive interventions can be used, such as "catching the child being good" by noticing and/or reinforcing the absence of aggressive behavior or the presence of cooperative behavior. A comprehensive behavior system can be set up by using a behavior chart to detail progress. Parents can be involved in establishing a home-based reward system that is contingent upon positive reports from school. In more extreme cases, it might be necessary to enlist the assistance of a tough authority person who has no problem imposing his or her thoughts and feelings, or even using restraint, if needed, upon the student exhibiting aggressive behavior.

In all cases, effective discipline with aggressive students also requires that we find safe ways of empowering them. These students need to learn and experience that they can feel adequate by influencing people and events around them. Regular opportunities to participate in the following kinds of activities can be a very effective deterrent to aggressive behavior:

- Ask the student to share an opinion: "Stanley, some students and teachers think it is too noisy in the cafeteria. What do you think?"

- Invite the student to solve a problem: "Linda, even though we have rules about not interrupting, I notice lots of students don't seem to follow through. How do you think we could fix this problem? If you were in charge, what would you do?"

- Ask the student to suggest an alternative consequence or action: "Bob, you and Steven keep getting into a hassle with each other. I'm sure he's at fault as well, but when I see you about to hit him, I need you to stop immediately. I don't want to embarrass you in the classroom, so give me some ideas that will get you to stop right away."

- Put the student in charge of a tough situation, and offer proper support: "Alma, lots of teachers are worried about bullying on the playground. In fact, some are even thinking that children should no longer be allowed outside to play during recess. We need some students like you who can keep your eye on things to make sure that bullying no longer happens. When you see someone being mean to somebody else, I'm hoping that you will politely ask that person to stop. If they don't, you can tell one of the playground supervisors who will then get involved. Can I count on you to help out in this way? By the way, do you have any other ideas that will stop bullying?"

- Ask the student to share a strength with others: "Victor, I know you love to play football. You have to be tough and smart to be a good football player. I was hoping that you could share your love of football with the class. How about telling us all the things you like most about the game?"

HELP POORLY ORGANIZED STUDENTS

Many students who act irresponsibly are poorly organized. They forget to bring books, often put assignments in the wrong folder, are not focused on time requirements, and have lockers or desks that look like a tornado struck them. If they take class notes, the notes are often chaotic or disjointed. Is it any wonder that many of these students become discouraged when they experience little academic success despite their adequate intelligence and academic skills? Many prefer becoming a discipline problem to feeling stupid. Poorly organized students can be helped in a variety of ways:

- If possible, provide the student with duplicate materials for home and school. The less movement there is of materials, the less likely they are to get lost.

- Provide a list of specific activities to be done and tape the list to the student's desk (with older students, suggest that they tape it to their own desks). Recommend that the student place a check mark next to each activity following completion.

- Write down each lesson's key objectives: "By the end of the lesson you will know who King Ferdinand and Queen Isabella were and how they contributed to Columbus' discoveries." Ask students to keep a journal of these objectives.

- Pair or team poorly organized students with well-organized students. Provide some class time for pairs or teams to ensure that everyone has the assignment and knows what needs to be done.

- Many poorly organized students are also easily distracted. If a student responds excessively to auditory distraction while working, suggest that he or she wear headphones to block out sound or listen to soothing music.

- When an assignment or portion of an assignment is successfully completed, congratulate the student, and try to get him or her to describe what was done to be successful. The more students attribute success to their own talents and resources, the more likely they are to realize that they already have what it takes to succeed.

- Reduce the quantity of material required. Poorly organized students can be better focused when there are fewer distractions. Put only a few problems on each page, with each succeeding page given only after the previous one has been completed.

- Have specific procedures and be precise in communicating them. Poorly organized students appreciate clarity of expectations. Be clear about such things as how to enter the room, where to find the work, what to do when the work is finished, where to find assignments, what to do if they realize they forgot an assignment when they get home, and how to get someone's attention.

- If you have email, make sure your students and their parents have your email address. Consider starting a website for your classes, and post notices, assignments, timelines, and other important exchanges and instructions there. The website is an excellent way to communicate with your students. Keep in mind that the material posted will not only be available to students, but to others as well: parents, guardians, other faculty members, and administrators. Be certain your students and their parents or guardians know the Internet address (URL) for your site. It can also be immensely helpful to have a daily or weekly online review of the conceptual highlights that you want your students to learn.

ENCOURAGE JOURNALING

Many students appreciate the opportunity to share their thoughts and feelings with a trusted adult, and often the trusted adult is, or can be, their teacher. Encourage your students to keep a journal they know will be occasionally handed in and read by their teacher. A journal can have many uses and be structured in several different ways. You can suggest that they make an entry in their journals when tensions are high. When an unbelievable event happens that triggers a major reaction, such as the World Trade Center attacks, or when the issues of daily living require expression, a journal can be a safe place for students to unload their concerns and anxieties. When the concern is shared by students and teacher, the teacher may ask a structured question such as, "What do you think can be done to make bullying less of a problem?" Another possibility is for students to make open-ended entries into their journals. Collect their journals periodically for examination and comment. If students prefer that you not read a specific portion, tell them to cover the entry with a blank sheet of paper attached with staples, for example. When students want you to pay careful attention to an entry, suggest that they highlight the part of the entry that they especially want you to find. A journal can be an effective, time-conserving way to make and sustain important personal connections with your students.

To begin journaling, you might suggest that students devote a special notebook for this purpose. Invite them to put pictures, words, or sayings on the outside that reflect who they are. Encourage them to write in their journals when tensions seem particularly high or when there is an important issue that is affecting them, especially in regard to your class.

USE A SUGGESTION BOX

Seeking student input is one of the best ways to demonstrate our respect of their ability to make good decisions. Encourage your students to share input by inviting them to write or draw suggestions that they believe will make the classroom a better place. Although it may feel risky to become open to criticism from our students, they often appreciate the opportunity to make the classroom a place where they can learn more effectively. Sometimes they come up with small suggestions that do not require much change but that lead to a much better climate for learning. Be sure that you remind them to express themselves in a respectful way. Our invitations for their suggestions can give us another opportunity to establish or re-establish boundaries. You might say:

> I am always interested in doing things that will help you learn, and feel better about being here. Whenever you have an idea that you think will make our classroom a better place, I hope you will either tell me at a time when I can listen (*name those times*) or write or draw your suggestions and put them in the suggestion box. After I read all of the suggestions, I will either adopt them or let you know why I think your suggestion will not work here. So, if you put your name on the suggestion, you have my guarantee that it will be read, and I will either use your suggestion or tell you why I don't think it would work in our classroom. I am always eager to make our class a better place. However, I do not want to be interrupted with suggestions or comments during the middle of class with statements such as, "This is boring," "When am I ever

going to use that?" and "I already learned this." So when you are truly serious about making our class a better place, your best chance of changing things around here is to either see me or write to me with your suggestions.

5 Tips for Motivating Students

If you listen long enough, people will explain how they can be motivated.

—Alan Loy McGinnis,
Achievement Authority and Author

MOTIVATE YOUR STUDENTS WITH PREFERRED LEARNING ACTIVITIES

Students often tell us how they best learn in a variety of ways. Howard Gardner and his followers have written several books in which they document the existence of multiple intelligences and suggest ways to modify the curriculum. Although many reasons have been offered to explain why people learn differently, and numerous classroom activities have been developed to address these learning differences, instruction in most American classrooms (most notably at the secondary level) is not much different today than it was 50 years ago. Observations of students suggest that their engagement with subject matter is much better when certain learning conditions or activities are present.

Students should be encouraged to build or draw things. Many students learn better from hands-on activities. For these students, try to use three-dimensional objects to illustrate the concepts you are teaching. For example, some students need to look at and touch a globe in order to relate to and place a location being studied. The mathematical concept of area becomes much clearer to some students when they can measure the actual locale of a familiar place.

Encourage students to make collections. John Goodlad (1984), in his book *A Place Called School: Promise for the Future,* reported that some of the students he interviewed had a preference for collecting, or making collections, as their learning activity. You can help similar students in your class by encouraging them to make collections. When students study the seasons of the year, ask them to collect different types of leaves. Concave versus convex objects can be collected, as can numerous other examples of concepts being presented to the students. Collections of items with greater or lesser resistance to gravity can make this abstract concept much easier to understand for many students.

Take students on field trips. A visit to a place can bring what was studied in the classroom to life and can enhance learning for a significant number of students. As a youngster, the Battle of Gettysburg came to life for me when I had an opportunity to visit the site. Observing Little Round Top gave me a much clearer understanding of that battle than all the reading I had previously done.

Ask students to interview people. Students are generally quite motivated with assignments that involve finding people who represent what is being studied. During a math lesson on making deductions, my daughter's assignment was to explore how one variable is related to another. She was asked to determine the thumb dominance of a sample of family and friends by having the selected group fold their hands on top of a desk with their fingers interlocked. The dominant thumb, she was told, is on top of the other. Her assignment was to record the finding of thumb dominance, determine if there is a relationship between hand and thumb dominance, and then write a sentence describing the relationship. I recall how curious and enthusiastic she became as she interviewed people about their hand dominance and then had them fold their hands.

Allow students to act things out. Dramatic skits that are designed to convey or consolidate information can easily blend multiple modes of learning. Debating opposing views of the same issue, pretending to be a character in a novel, and having students develop a skit that conveys main themes they have learned in a unit are just a few of many possibilities.

Ask students to work cooperatively. Many teachers have found students prefer to work on projects with others. There has been much written over the years about cooperative learning. Essentially, it is important for the teacher to decide on the goal(s) of a learning activity and then use the goals as a guide in structuring group composition and roles so that each group member will contribute to the group's success. In addition to structuring the subject matter the group addresses, the group may need to be structured by assigning or having students choose typical roles within the group such as timekeeper, directions-repeater, noise monitor, and scribe.

Promote special theme day. Having dress-up or dress-down days can be stimulating fun that makes students and educators want to come to school. To promote the school play, drama students at my daughter's middle school wore pajamas on the day of the first performance. At first, I thought it silly and inappropriate for pajamas to be worn to school, but I changed my mind when I saw the enthusiasm and energy it aroused in my daughter and her friends.

Use motivating music. Every generation is motivated by music, and occasionally playing their music in the background can be invigorating for them. At other times you might play "easy listening" or soothing classical music which can have a calming effect. You might even allow your students to present oral reports in a musical way. Even better, present some of your concepts with the assistance of music. Aaron Nolan, a special-education teacher in Henrietta, New York, has composed a variety of songs to teach science concepts to his special-education students. One of the songs is reprinted with permission below.

DNA Bells

by Aaron Nolan
(Sing to the tune of "Jingle Bells.")

DNA, DNA:
Double helix shape
Made from many nucleotides
Sugar, base, and **phosphate.**

RNA, RNA
Has only one strand.
It acts as the messenger
To give DNA a hand.

Dashing through the cell
In a one-stranded RNA
O'er the fields we go
Singing about DNA.

DNA has two strands—
It also has thymine
Made of the nucleotides:
'Tis the reason your cells work so fine.

Oh! DNA, DNA:
Double helix shape
Made from many nucleotides
Sugar, base, and **phosphate.**

RNA, RNA
Has only one strand.
It acts as the messenger
To give DNA a hand.

ELIMINATE THE LANGUAGE OF FAILURE

Let your students know you understand that school is easier for some than for others. Often, students who are thought of as smart in school are those who seem to be good at everything. Yet in life outside of school, it is rare that an individual shines at everything, and it is unnecessary for people to achieve success in every element of their lives. It is important to convey this to our students, particularly when they struggle with learning certain subjects. We want our students to hear our main message: "While it is understandable that many people feel like giving up when things become difficult, everyone can get better at anything by making an effort." No one is going to be the best at everything, so the challenge is to become as good as you can at what you do.

Confront students when you hear the language of failure and refuse to allow such talking to continue. Make a point of challenging self-directed put-downs that destroy motivation. In your classrooms, ban the use of certain harmful words and phrases. Contrast failure beliefs with success beliefs, such as:

- "I can't" *(failure belief)* becomes "I haven't yet" *(success belief)*.

- "It's too hard" *becomes* "It isn't easy, but I will get it."

- "I am unable" *becomes* "I need to try harder."

- "This is impossible to figure out" *becomes* "I will ask for help and keep trying."

You might also consider posting inspirational messages and credos in the classroom—messages that challenge your students to believe that most things are possible. For example, when Thomas Edison's quest to invent a light bulb failed for the 500th time, he was asked if he felt like a failure. His response was to say that since he now knew the 500 experiments that were unsuccessful, he could only be closer than ever to a solution that would work.

Miguel Rodriguez, a math teacher of alternative students in a barrio of Houston, Texas, has developed the following Student/Teacher Credo. Miguel said that at first his students laughed and dismissed the message, but through repetition most students have become prideful. It is truly inspirational to watch Miguel lead his students as they chant the following in unison at the beginning of each class:

I'm a believer, not a doubter.

I'm a dreamer, not a sleeper.

I'm above, not below.

I'm smart, not slow.

I'm the head, not the tail.

I can do math, 'cause I practice math.

I can do anything that my heart desires.

I work hard.

I play hard.

And I treat people how I want to be TREATED.

I'm powerful, I'm powerful, I'm POWERFUL!

You might consider posting the motivating inspirational messages that appear on the next two pages.

What a bright idea you had in class today!

Thanks for sharing it with us!

© 2005 Allen Mendler

I spy good work habits.

KEEP IT UP!

You set a great example for others!

© 2005 Allen Mendler

Your improved behavior is out of this world!

I appreciate it— THANKS!

© 2005 Allen Mendler

It bugs me when you talk out of turn.

Please be considerate of me
and your classmates.

© 2005 Allen Mendler

It brightens my day
when you follow the rules!

THANKS SO MUCH!

© 2005 Allen Mendler

SURPRISE YOUR STUDENTS, AND GIVE THEM APPROVAL WHEN THEY DO NOT EXPECT IT

Offer unexpected appreciation to your students regularly because words of encouragement and admiration really make kids feel special. When returning papers to your students, you could also include a personal message that commends them. For example, a teacher I recently met will write a note like the following on a separate sheet of paper: "Aaron, you are one of the reasons I enjoy teaching." She usually times her message to be received when she sees or senses that a student is making an extraordinary effort to improve some aspect of his or her behavior or attitude. Other possibilities for words of encouragement:

- I just want you to know your improved behavior is making my day.

- I enjoy watching you have a good day.

- You hung in there even though the work was hard. I am impressed.

- Your effort paid off. Congratulations!

- Keep up the good work.

- Your improvement is a joy to see. Keep it up.

- This is one terrific paper!

- It looks like coming in early for extra help is really paying off.

You might think of the kinds of things colleagues, administrators, or parents say or do that make you feel special and consider how you might share similar messages with your students.

HOMEWORK SUGGESTIONS

I sometimes think that if we eliminated buses and homework, 90% of what we call discipline problems would go away. In a substantial number of our schools, the struggle to get students to do their homework often feels like a lost battle. Poor grades are often directly related to missing homework. Even when students do well on tests and other measures of competence, substantial penalties are usually imposed for incomplete or missing homework. For a variety of reasons, doing homework is simply not valued, nor is it a priority among too many students. Some have discovered that not doing homework is an effective way to frustrate their parents and teachers.

Many caring parents feel like they have to continually police their children in order to monitor their homework efforts. There is little else that makes teachers feel more frequently helpless on a regular basis than students who refuse to do their homework. Since homework usually counts for a considerable portion of a student's grade, many capable students wind up doing poorly in classes despite their mastery of the material. To complicate matters even more, there is considerable controversy within the educational literature as to how useful homework actually is in improving mastery of material. In general, there is not much evidence to suggest that homework benefits learning throughout the elementary years. There is better support, although still weak, of the relationship between achievement and homework during middle school. The strongest evidence for the benefits of homework is during the high school years. High school students who do the greatest amount of homework are the strongest learners (Muhlenbruck, Cooper, Nye, & Lindsay, 2000). Although there are no sure-fire ways of getting students to do their homework, the following suggestions can help.

Relate the assignment to what is covered in class. Do not make homework a time for students to do something that was not introduced during class. Make it a time for practice and going into greater depth. Go over the homework assignment, and be sure it applies and relates to the current lesson. Many students perceive homework that is collected but not integrated in class activities as a waste of their time.

Assign a proper amount of homework. Homework should not exceed 10 minutes for each grade level. A first grader should get 10 minutes (at most) while a seventh grader should get no more than 70 minutes worth of homework.

Plan homework in collaboration with other teachers when possible. The goal of homework should be to support learning. Good learning becomes impossible when there is too much dissimilar information given by too many sources at the same time. If students have a major math test in a week, it is unwise to burden them with an assignment to write a lengthy essay. Educators need time to plan together, and when possible, to team-teach so that this kind of information can flow more freely.

Encourage students to work together while doing their assignments. Many educators complain about how much students socialize when they are supposed to be studying. Yet most research on young people finds that many spend too many hours interacting with non-living objects such as computers and Nintendo games. Even when they communicate with each other outside of school, instant messaging is more typical than face-to-face interaction. Make an effort to assign projects that encourage cooperation and coordination. In life outside of school, people more often work together than alone.

Let students know where they can get help if they do not understand the homework. Effective homework assignments should include specifics on how students can get help when they need it. It can be discouraging for students to make an effort, encounter a problem they do not understand, and have nowhere to turn for help. Even many highly educated and involved parents have a difficult time helping their children beyond fifth grade. When students know where they can get the help they need, they are more likely to do their homework in a sustained way. Help your students arrange "study buddies." Be sure that each student has the names of two or three others. If they encounter a problem, they can call one or more of their buddies. If possible, establish a homework hotline that is staffed either by teachers or advanced students. If difficulty in understanding a problem occurs, for example, students can call the hotline for assistance. You might even consider placing a page on the school's website with information or instructions for students should they need assistance with homework material. This could include directions, clarifications, who to call for help, and answers to the most frequently asked questions.

Grade and return homework quickly. It is disrespectful and unhelpful to return homework long after it was handed in. Any feedback or improvement you hope to give a student is most meaningful within the first 3 days after completing the assignment. After that time, there is little relevance of homework to improvement.

Clearly advise your students of the homework objectives. Just as an effective classroom is driven by learning objectives, homework is also most effective when students know the bigger purpose served by it. It is best to not only tell your students what they have to do for homework, but to also spend a few minutes helping them understand what they are expected to achieve as a result: "After completing your homework tonight, you should be able to explain three reasons why objects filled with helium float." People tend to be more productive when they not only know what to do, but also why they should do it.

Make homework optional for students who do not need the practice. Find ways of showing the benefits of doing homework. For example, you might tell students that there will be an assignment every night in order for them to practice what has been learned. Individual students can then do as much or as little work as they feel necessary depending upon how well they believe they know the material. Explain that you will be giving quick quizzes several times each week to test them on their knowledge so that you can be sure they are mastering the material. Meet with those students who do not do well on the quizzes to explore how they can do their homework more effectively.

Give extra credit for doing homework. Some schools have a critical mass of students who do not or will not do homework for a variety of reasons. Rather than getting into constant power struggles, it can be more effective to make homework an extra-credit option. Students might "bank" points that they get for homework to use on tests.

Give the students homework choices and options. Students are more receptive to assignments that offer them choices. We can give students the choice of how to accomplish the assignment. For example, tell them they can write an essay or give a presentation. If there are eight problems, ask them to turn in the answers for the five problems that they think will best prove their understanding of the material.

Think of homework as a gift. A high-school algebra teacher said that a greater number of her students began to turn in more of their homework when she began to treat and speak of homework as a gift rather than an expectation.

Make homework completion a game.
In one middle school I visited, the teacher had a homework strategy that effectively used class rewards in a fun way to dramatically increase homework production. The word "homework" was written with each letter H-O-M-E-W-O-R-K on a separate 8½ × 11 sheet of paper. Each day a letter was revealed when all of the students turned in their homework. When the word was completely spelled, the class earned a party for one class period.

part 3

Tips for Intervention

6 Tips for Handling Tough Moments

> *When students challenge our authority, it takes professionalism to know not only what to do but how to do it in a dignified way.*
>
> —Barbara Mendler, Educator

LEARN NOT TO TAKE OFFENSIVE BEHAVIOR PERSONALLY

Mrs. Kendall asked Shirelle to stop talking to her buddy, and Shirelle angrily responded, "F--- off!" Mrs. Kendall replied, "Shirelle, you are obviously having a horrible day. I wish I could help you but I can't right now, so can you collect yourself, or do you need to leave for a few minutes?" Shirelle continued, "Damned right I am having a lousy day. I haven't seen my old man in months, and my mom has cancer. You'd be having a bad day too if you were in my shoes!" Mrs. Kendall said, "You're absolutely right, Shirelle, and my heart aches for you. But I must remind you that I didn't cause these things to happen, and I don't deserve that kind of language. We'll talk later." Shirelle soon apologized for her outburst.

Getting past aggressive, angering moments may be the greatest challenge we face in being able to work successfully with difficult students. For Mrs. Kendall to respond as she did, she had to find strength within herself so that she could stay in charge of a moment that easily could have exploded. Nowadays, all educators have students who face huge and often overwhelming issues in their lives. It is not uncommon for these students to lash out at whoever happens to be around as a way of expressing frustrations, disappointments, and sorrows. To stay engaged with such students, it is necessary that we find ways of maintaining our personal connection to them without taking their offensive behavior personally. Only in this way was Mrs. Kendall able to avoid an understandable knee-jerk reaction that might have led her to a predictable fight or flight response. And neither fight nor flight is desirable when working with students we see on a daily basis. Getting beyond fight or flight can be an extremely difficult thing to do since a driving force in becoming a teacher, administrator, or youth worker is having a caring, sensitive manner—and caring, sensitive people tend to react vigorously to hurtful, offensive behavior. Handling tough moments effectively, such as those faced by Mrs. Kendall, requires almost superhuman effort.

It can help to think of yourself as being two persons as a way to sustain a caring and engaging manner when your buttons are pushed. The first person is the man or woman on the street within you who has unique preferences, values, friends, and family members. Outside of school, most difficult students who say or do offensive things are not people that we would want to spend time with. Yet on "company time" it is necessary that we become the second person who must work to avoid rejecting these students with knee-jerk reactions of anger and vindictiveness. Our obligation as educators requires that we work with all students. The goal with difficult students should be to make it as hard as possible for them to throw their education away.

One way to avoid a knee-jerk reaction of anger when students use offensive behaviors is to try hearing inappropriate language in neutral or even comic ways. For example, imagine you have just heard a student say something to you that is personally offensive. Naturally, you would feel angry, but for a moment use your imagination to replace your memory of the vulgar words with inoffensive or even comic words, such as "computer," "apple," or even "ceiling tile." You would not be offended if a student called you a truck, would you? The answer is obvious, and if a student called you a truck, you would most probably be concerned that the student had lost touch with reality. When faced with such situations as verbal disrespect, our main focus should remain on the student in an effort to find a way of getting that student some help. This is the work that is so very important for us to do, and we must not permit knee-jerk reactions that perpetuate ugly conflict to overtake us.

Only by first defusing ourselves can we create a buffer between the offensive behavior and the counter-aggressive reaction. We must be confident in our ability to handle tough moments. A teacher at one of my seminars recalled an incident in which she made a request of a student. The student answered saying, "F--- you." Remaining calm, the teacher effectively defused the situation by firmly stating, "That was not one of the choices." Another teacher told a story about a boy who was determined to make her quit her job. He said, "I'm gonna push your buttons so that eventually you are gonna quit. I know I can do that because I've done it to other teachers." Maintaining concern for the student without taking things personally, this teacher said, "You probably have the power to make my life miserable. I wonder if I have the power to make your life successful. Tell me, is the only success you know in school to make the lives of teachers miserable? I'll tell you this: I don't know you well enough to know what else you can achieve, but I'm not giving up on you no matter what!"

USE P.E.P. FOR CONSEQUENCE IMPLEMENTATION

It has long been known that how we carry ourselves—our demeanor or bearing—is more important than what we say. A good friend and outstanding educator, Colleen Zawadzki, in paraphrasing her karate sensei, advises that teachers need to "act as if they own the sidewalk on which they walk and are planning to buy the other side." At no time is this demeanor more necessary than when defusing an angry student or when implementing consequences. It is necessary to clearly and assertively convey leadership in a dignified manner when rules are being challenged. In most cases, this is best done by correcting a student while getting as close to the offender as possible (**P**roximity), making eye contact (**E**ye contact), and with as much **P**rivacy as is realistic in the public setting of a classroom. In addition, as students become louder, it is most effective for the teacher to become quieter in voice. Using P.E.P. helps students "save face" because they are not embarrassed in front of their peers when they allow the teacher to take charge.

P.E.P. requires caution since some students—either for personal, cultural, or emotional reasons—have less tolerance for physical closeness or eye contact than other students. Considering this, there is no substitute for use of good judgment. Although P.E.P. works well early in a conflict, it is far less effective and may even provoke greater conflict when a student is already highly volatile. There are times when it is best to avoid verbal correction with P.E.P. and instead use nonverbal P.E.P. To do this, the teacher or administrator approaches the student and leaves a written or graphic message on a self-stick note or an index card that can be clearly understood by the student. (See sample P.E.P. notes on the next page. More elaborate P.E.P. types of statements appear on pages 81 and 82.) Finally, using P.E.P. for behavior works most effectively when against the backdrop of students knowing that there are many "up-close and personal" interactions that teachers have with them. It is therefore extremely important to make P.E.P. a regular part of how you perform each day in the classroom. Every corrective message should ideally be balanced with at least three or four encouraging, positive comments. When we move around the room regularly while making formal and informal contact with students, this style of interacting with them makes it less noticeable when P.E.P. is being used for purposes of correction, thereby helping a difficult student save face. Nobody wants to look like a "loser" in front of others, so helping students save face when conflict occurs is a very important goal in defusing a power struggle.

HANDLE POWER STRUGGLES STEP-BY-STEP

If students challenge your authority in the classroom during instructional time, the following step-by-step sequence will help.

Refuse to always stop class to deal with each incident of misbehavior. During a relatively calm moment in which nobody is challenging your authority, let your students know that you will not be stopping class to deal with each incident of misbehavior. You might say, "We have been spending too much time lately reminding people about their behavior and not enough time on what needs to be learned. From now on, it may sometimes look to you as if I am ignoring someone when rules are broken because I will not always stop what we are all doing to deal with someone who is having a hard time behaving. Instead, I will meet with that student later, and we will figure out a proper consequence." Then, at some later time when something inappropriate happens, it is effective to say, "I know that everybody heard what Joey just said, and most of you are probably wondering what I am going to do about it. Later on, when I get a moment with him, we will figure out what the problem is and what we will do about it. Anyway, as far as today's lesson goes . . ."

Use P.E.P. Try to defuse the student privately, with eye contact and close proximity. Be sure to lower and calm your voice as the student becomes louder.

Agree with a complaint and redirect it. When students complain about something publicly, agree that they have a right to their point of view, but remind them that there is a proper time and place for everything. If a student complains that things are boring, you might say, "Joey, you have a right to feel the way you do, but after class is the proper time for us to discuss how the class might be made more interesting. I'll look forward to seeing you at that time."

Acknowledge the student's power. If a student publicly tells you that you cannot make him or her behave, it is usually best to agree as a way of defusing the incident. We all need to believe that we have power and influence, and students who continually trigger power struggles in public are virtually always struggling with this issue. Simply say to the student, "You are absolutely right. I cannot make you do anything against your will. Only you have the power to decide, and I hope you make a good choice. Anyway class, I think we were on page 53, number 2. . . ." When necessary, follow up after class with the student by either implementing a consequence or having the student develop a plan for less public outbursts in the future.

Identify what is at stake if the power struggle continues. A very effective way to defuse a situation is to let the student know that power struggles rarely solve problems because they eventually make everyone involved look bad. You might say to the student, "Leah, I find myself getting mad, and I think you are, too. If we continue this here and now, we are going to have an argument that neither one of us wants to lose. I am not going to look bad in front of everybody, and I know you don't want to look bad either. We'll continue this after class. I look forward to seeing you then."

Have a student who is acting particularly difficult teach the class. It is rarely necessary, but a role reversal with a student while you are caught in the middle of a conflict can be extremely effective for dealing with power struggles. This is most appropriate for the rare times when a targeted student is making it so difficult that it is virtually impossible for you to keep teaching and for other students to continue learning. It is also a good method to consider using if other students begin to misbehave, and you feel like you have a "doomed instructional moment." For example, say, "John, I will not try to shout louder than you. Since I can no longer teach, maybe you can do a better job. Keep us on the topic. Anything goes other than 'class dismissed!'" Most students will back off at this point, although some will make a final comment such as, "I'm not going to teach this stupid class." If this happens, it is usually best to back off from the conflict and resume teaching. Some students will escalate the situation by becoming even more inappropriate in language or gesture. If you ignore them at this point, you can usually regain the instructional moment sooner. If a student actually takes you up on your invitation and starts teaching, act as if you are the disruptive student. Some students need to actually experience the effects of their own behavior in order to become aware of how inappropriate they are. Meet later with the student to either implement a consequence or develop a plan.

React unexpectedly. Teresa Doherty, a ninth-grade teacher, shared an incident in which an apparently frustrated student in her class called her an extremely foul-mouthed and objectionable name. She defused the conflict by saying, "Your language is totally inappropriate. Now what is it that you are trying to tell me?"

The use of inappropriate language and gestures by students towards teachers and administrators has become far too common. Clearly, standards of civility need to be reaffirmed and enforced at school. Yet equally important is that educators learn not to react too emotionally when our buttons are pushed. It is important that we work to defuse ourselves when we are angry so that we can respond with good judgment to offensive behavior. Our goal should be to take charge of the situation immediately after it occurs. It can sometimes be extremely effective to react unemotionally and unexpectedly in a highly charged atmosphere. For example, in the movie *Roxanne,* the Cyrano character (played by Steve Martin) sits at a bar and is mercilessly teased about his huge nose. Cyrano counters every put-down by poking even more fun at himself, and eventually his provocateurs embrace him as a buddy once they realize that he can stand up to them.

I was recently told about a small, elderly middle-school teacher who took a boy out into the hall and told him to cool off for 5 minutes, and then return to class. As she was turning around to re-enter the classroom, the student flipped her off with his middle finger. She turned back towards him and said, "Maybe you misunderstood. I said to take 5 minutes *(holding up five fingers)*, not 1 *(as she held up her middle finger)*." Nothing more was said.

Use three powerful words that defuse. In most instances it is sufficient to confront the student by saying, "I feel disrespected." Usually, this is sufficient to get students to back off, but if not, then follow up with "Is that what you meant?" Most students will say no. To the few who say yes, conclude with, "Then I am sorry if I have done something upsetting to you. After class, we'll find a solution."

Meet with the student afterward and discuss the incident further or implement consequence(s). Closure to difficult moments can often be achieved by meeting with the student after the incident. The goal should be to explore how to prevent the problem from reoccurring. If it was atypical behavior from a student and entirely out of character, then the primary emphasis should be to offer support for any stress in the student's life. For example, one might say, "Raj, we both know your language was unacceptable today, but what most concerns me is that you were just not being yourself. If there are some things in your life bothering you, I'm wondering what they are so I might better understand what is going on." If the problem is chronic, then working to elicit a plan for better behavior is the recommended choice. Finally, if there was a major scene in class, you might implement "visible" consequences, such as, "Leila, I hope this doesn't happen again, and I'm glad that you see the error of your ways. Nonetheless, I am going to submit a referral and expect something like a detention to occur because I want to make sure that everybody understands that this kind of behavior is entirely unacceptable and has consequences."

Use a third party. When conflicts keep occurring between yourself and a student or small group of students, you might want to ask a third party to assist in helping everyone involved to find a good solution (see "Positive Student Confrontation" on page 103).

QUICK ONE-LINERS—WHAT I SHOULD SAY WHEN . . .

There are many things that can be said to defuse difficult situations and to gain the respect of your students. Once again, the key is to refuse taking offensive behavior personally. Most power struggles are fueled by the desire of both the teacher and the student to save face. Neither wants to look bad. Here is the conundrum: Teachers and administrators cannot afford to look like wimps if we are to gain the respect of our students, and the student involved in the power struggle is afraid of losing the respect of his peers if he backs down. Effective one-liners are designed to stop the problem while maintaining the teacher's authority and everyone's dignity as much as possible. In deciding which of these responses is best for you, it is helpful for you to actually imagine various situations in which a student or group of students says or does something that you consider to be inappropriate. Then try in your own mind to make the situation come back to life, and practice using the sentence or sentences that best fit the moment. It is sometimes necessary to do this several times before you find the response(s) that will be most useful.

Quick One-Liners That Can End Conflict and Preserve Everyone's Dignity

- Wow, I had no idea you felt that way. Tell me more at a later time.

- I'm sorry you feel that way.

- I must have done something to bug you, but now is not a good time for me. Let's talk later.

- Let me see if I understand you correctly. You are telling me _____. Is that right?

(continued)

- I feel disrespected. Is that what you meant? *(Refer to "Use Three Powerful Words That Defuse" on page 99.)*

- You are just not yourself today, so I am going to let that slide right now rather than get into a hassle about it.

- When you are ready to speak in an appropriate tone, I'll be happy to listen.

- I use those kinds of words when I am really upset about something. I'm sorry you feel upset right now.

- You present an interesting opinion.

- If I allowed you to do that, I'd be showing no respect. I will respect you even when you show little respect for yourself.

- I am concerned. If you do _____, trouble will follow: *(State the consequences if you know what they are)*. You don't need that.

- You might be right about that.

- Someday I will, but that doesn't solve the problem, does it?

- I don't appreciate being talked to in that way.

- The choice is yours, and you can change your mind if you want.

- We need some time to look into this because I'd like to learn more about what you mean. Now is not a good time.

- Your language is totally unacceptable. What is it that you really want to say?

- I wish you weren't so angry. After you calm down, I want to understand what is bothering you.

- I must have done something to really hurt you. I'm sorry if that happened.

(continued)

- Even though I like to be liked, I'm here to teach you and not to be liked by you.

- I am really concerned! It is very important that I understand why you are so mad. Please tell me later when I can really listen.

- Now is not a good time for me to tell you. I know it is hard to wait, but thanks for hanging in there.

- Let me see if I understand this correctly. . . .

- I guess you and I see this differently. Let's try to find a solution after class.

- When you are ready to talk rather than yell, I'll be more than happy to listen to you.

- Wow, you must be really mad to want to embarrass me like that in front of everyone. It makes me want to fight back, but then we'd never solve this problem.

- I want to understand why you are so annoyed. But hitting and swearing don't help. Let's talk later so that I can really understand.

- Believe it or not, you are not the only one who has ever thought that.

- Later on, I hope you tell me exactly what is *(stupid, dumb)* about _____ so that we can fix it.

- Not now, but maybe some other time.

- I forgive you for losing your temper. What can you do to not need forgiveness again?

- Now is not a good time to deal with this. I'm available at _____ *(name times).*

Many challenging students can be defused by giving requests or demands along with a simple, assertive "please" followed by "thanks": "Please raise your hand. Thanks. Please move along. Thanks." Laura Kress, a teacher at Wells Middle School in Spring, Texas, ends requests by thanking difficult students. For example, she will say to a very agitated student, "Thanks for walking away when you were so angry. It takes a lot to do that."

Keep in mind that at least 85 to 90% of our message is communicated by tone of voice and body language. Although the sentences above can certainly help, even more important is for our attitude to convey firmness and respectfulness. Try to practice remaining calm in the face of challenging moments while firmly saying what you mean.

POSITIVE STUDENT CONFRONTATION

Using a third party mediator is often helpful in resolving conflict between two or more parties. Since the writing of *Discipline With Dignity* (Curwin & Mendler, 1988, 1999), many schools have developed peer mediation and conflict resolution programs in which students are trained to act as a facilitator when conflict occurs between other students. Our approach, called Positive Student Confrontation, is designed as a conflict resolution process that can be used to deal with student-to-student conflict or student-to-teacher conflict. The process begins with a neutral third party mediator who we call the "coach" (a teacher, administrator, counselor, or student). The coach meets with those in conflict and takes them through the following steps:

1. The coach describes the problem, process, and his or her role: "I understand that there are some things that are getting in the way for each of you. I'm here to see if I can help you both find a way to feel better about being together at school."

2. The coach encourages each person to share his or her feelings of dislike, resentment, anger, or frustration: "This may not be easy, but I want both of you to tell what the other (he or she) says or does that you dislike."

3. After each person states his or her dislikes, the coach asks the other person to repeat or paraphrase the other's statements. This encourages an understanding of each other's concerns. (Paraphrasing should be used in subsequent steps as well.)

4. The coach encourages each person to share what he or she likes or appreciates about the other: "This might be really difficult since the two of you are here because of a problem, but I want you each to think hard about what you like or appreciate about each other. Then tell each other what you think." This step can help people in conflict begin to soften their positions.

5. The coach encourages each person to make demands: "Tell what you want *(name the person)* to do differently from what he or she is doing right now."

6. The coach encourages negotiation: "From what you have heard *(name the person)* say, explain what you are willing to do differently that you think could help solve this problem."

7. Partial or full agreement is reached, put in writing, and signed.

8. Responsibilities for evaluation are established so that each side can keep track of how well the agreement is working.

9. A follow-up meeting is scheduled within a few days to assess progress.

As the coach, it is important to be aware that both sides usually come with a list of complaints that feeds their frustrations. When there are numerous complaints, the coach needs to ask each side to list only the three or four things that they most want to see changed. That makes the mediation more manageable, as it is both practical and desirable to have both sides succeed in committing to small but clear changes that can be a building block for future negotiation of remaining concerns.

WALK, TALK, AND MOVE WHEN PROBLEM-SOLVING WITH ACTIVE OR AGGRESSIVE STUDENTS

Active students tend to think best when they are in motion. This has many implications for instruction and discipline. I know a high-school teacher who gives out vinyl cushions (such as those used for comfort at ballgames) to discourage rocking. He tells students that he cannot permit rocking because they might fall and get hurt and he would then be in trouble. At the same time, he tells them he understands that not everybody can sit in a hard chair for a long time and concentrate, and though this technique may not be as therapeutic as rocking, they can wiggle around in their cushioned seats as much as they like. Rocking has dramatically decreased in his class.

Another high-school special-education teacher swapped exercise balls for chairs and found that his students were much better focused during sit-and-listen instruction. An elementary teacher told of much success in redirecting aggressive behaviors by tying a bungee cord around the chair legs of her extremely active students. Many of these students were habitually hitting, pushing, and even kicking each other. A bungee cord is elastic and durable, and she encourages them to kick, push, or pull the cord whenever they need to be active. The result has been a dramatic reduction of inappropriate behaviors between students.

I have observed that most angry students have a hard time expressing their feelings when they are really hot under the collar. They do best when they are allowed to cool down in a quiet place by taking a walk and reflecting upon what happened. They generally do not do as well when they are expected to sit and think about what they did and what they could have done differently. If these findings were applied to detentions and time-outs, kids would spend relatively brief intervals sitting and a lot more time moving (such as taking a supervised walk with a caring adult who could guide them through a problem-solving process for any future encounters).

HANDLING SLEEPY STUDENTS

A simple solution to the problem of sleepy students is to allow movement. Approach the student and say, "I know you are sleepy, so I'll let you go back, take a stretch, and return when you are ready. The only thing we need to figure out is how you can get up and move around without disturbing other students." If this behavior persists, it would be wise to suggest an evaluation to help determine the cause. There might be a medical condition, nutritional issue, drug concern, or other higher-valued priorities that lead to lack of sleep. Before an evaluation is completed, it is sensible to meet privately with the student and attempt to develop a plan to determine how he or she can stay awake in the class or how you can awaken the student without startling or embarrassing him or her. You might say:

> Betsy, I appreciate you making the effort to come to class. I understand how tired you are, but when I see students asleep I become distracted, and this makes it hard for me to concentrate on teaching. Further, I worry that you won't learn the material you need to know. How do you think we might solve this problem?

If the student offers little constructive help, you might arrange to share a signal with the student that you can use to awaken him or her without embarrassment. Be straightforward with the student concerning this: "Betsy, it is not my goal to embarrass you or make you feel uncomfortable. Let's figure out a way that I can get you to open your eyes in class in case you can't keep them open yourself." Finally, if the student offers no alternatives, propose some options that you can live with that also include humor and encourage choice-making: "In my mind, I could tap you on the shoulder, tap your desk, drum my fingers on your desk, or drop a heavy book on your head. Which would work best for you?"

It can also be helpful to have a noiseless fan that softly blows a breeze on the sleeping student. If weather permits, even a gentle natural breeze that comes in through the window from the outside would work just as well. Finally, one elementary teacher shared that she left a sleeping student in the classroom while she took the others to recess. She left a note on the student's desk that said, "We need to be awake to go to recess. Join us when you wake up." (Naturally, it would be important to provide adequate supervision for the child in this case.)

ASK "MIND-SHIFT" QUESTIONS WHEN A STUDENT IS LOSING CONTROL

When a student is highly provoked or out of control, we can help the student regain control by asking "mind-shift" questions. Mind-shift questions have basic, unemotional content that is completely unrelated to whatever might be the source of the student's agitated state. These questions are designed to defuse the student quickly. For example, if a student is having a tantrum, you might ask, "What did you have for breakfast today?" This question is designed to reduce arousal and refocus the student. Typically, the student will answer with a pause in the outburst before saying, "Why are you asking me that?" You can then say, "Because now I have your attention. Before, you were too mad to listen. So what did you have for breakfast today?" Any personally neutral or positively flavored question can serve the mind-shift function. Questions with a food theme are often effective. Other possibilities are:

- What's on TV tonight?
- Who won the game yesterday?
- Where is your favorite place to visit?
- What do you like to see at the mall?
- What position do you like to play?
- How did you put that model together?
- How are you able to draw so many good pictures?
- Do you like Coke® or Pepsi®?
- Which basketball team do you want to play for someday?
- What are you doing after school?
- What colors do you see?

Another mind-shift strategy is to use a phrase repeatedly as an anchor to a place of self-control, such as, "Excuse me—I need your focus right now."

7 Tips for Handling Difficult Situations

When students become out of control, it is important to take charge of the situation by remaining calm and implementing a crisis plan. Each classroom should have a crisis plan to address behaviors such as tantrums and fights. It is best to outline in advance what everyone is supposed to do when such an event takes place. Key factors determining the specifics of a crisis plan are the teacher's skills, where the event takes place, and the availability of other human resources for help when necessary. Ideally, all educators should receive training in crisis management that includes verbal and physical skills because such ability may be necessary to defuse the crisis. In reality, not everyone has experienced such training and even those who have vary in their effectiveness. It is therefore important for educators to know what to do in a crisis. Keep in mind that the sole goal during a crisis is to restore order when chaos is occurring.

HANDLING EXTREMES OF BEHAVIOR

You need to address three main areas to be prepared to handle extremes of behavior.

Identify What You Expect Students to Do

Let students know that you expect them to stay away from danger. At most, you will want them to assist by getting help. Explain and practice how they should respond when someone loses control or is having "an especially bad day." Work out a strategy that ensures you will receive assistance if student behavior is out of control. For example, it is advisable to have a special color-coded "pass" that is taken by a predetermined student (an errand runner) to a helper (an administrator, safety officer, or teacher) when the student receives the signal from the teacher needing assistance. You should establish a special code such as a sound or word that cannot be confused with any other. When you express the code, students will spring to action according to the plan that has been defined. The code is best reserved for the most extreme situations that would require students to leave the classroom for their own safety. Be sure to practice how you want them to act in such a crisis so that if the real moment occurs, they are ready.

It is wise for teachers to establish their classrooms with all students having a "responsible job." Just as one student may pass out papers while another is the line leader for a week, a student is assigned the job of "errand runner" and is responsible for going to the office with the pass. This job can be assumed on a rotating basis with all students being eligible as long as they understand the directions and demonstrate their knowledge while role-playing. If the teacher has any concerns that a student may not be ready to react quickly, a back-up child can be selected so that there is never any doubt about what needs to be done when the signal is given.

When dangerous behaviors such as fighting are widespread, holding the group accountable can be very effective. Consequences are recommended for those *observing* the fight in addition to those who are actually fighting. Since fights never occur in isolation and gain much of their steam because of audience participation, students need to know that they will experience consequences if they remain in the presence of those who are fighting. Even minor consequences such as a detention for observers can be a very effective deterrent. Most students who are not fighting but who are observing will not want to experience consequences for their presence. An inner-city school reported a significant reduction in fighting among students after they equipped all staff with instant cameras. Faculty members were asked to simply take pictures of anybody in close proximity of the fight. Students were advised that there would be disciplinary action taken against any students who appeared in the photographs. The result was that most students quickly scattered when teachers began taking pictures. By holding bystanders responsible, the message was sent that we are all important in making our school a safe place.

Identify What You Expect of Yourself

Assure your students that you will be the primary person who will deal with the out-of-control situation. For example, if a student is throwing a temper tantrum, you are the primary person who will be involved. Knowing and using verbal and physical calming techniques can be very helpful during these times.

Identify Specific Helpers for Support

This might be the most important category of all. It may be necessary that other trained adults assist in handling extreme situations. Be sure to identify who you will seek help from, how you will request assistance from the helper, and where you will turn if the identified helper is unavailable.

TURN EXCUSES INTO ACTIONS

Some students seek attention through displays of inadequacy. Behaviors such as continuous questioning along with comments such as, "I can't do it," "I did my best," or "I really tried, but I didn't know how to do it," are frequent. Students who become adept at trying but not achieving have often found an effective manipulative method that usually results in "trying the nerves" of people around them. When students claim they have tried hard, but there seems to be little evidence to back this up, challenge them respectfully. Tell them that you want to see exactly what was tried and what was accomplished. It may be necessary to create layers of "help" for these students in order to prevent them from not accomplishing their work or from placing an immediate demand upon you to help them. For example, you might tell a student that if he or she is unsure of what to do, the first thing is to take a minute and re-read the directions. If still unsure, the student can then ask as many as two "help" buddies. Finally, the student can come to you if he or she still does not understand what is required.

Focus on accepting what students do rather than what they tried. When a student says, "I tried," say to them, "Show me how." Ask them to explain precisely what they did, and if the excuse-making is more about blaming others (such as, "He made me do it"), tell the student that you are sure there were others who contributed but conclude by asking, "What did *you* do?" Joe Herman, an administrator in Wilmington, Delaware, uses powerful imagery involving guns and bullets with his challenging students when they blame teachers for their problems. He tells them, "You say that this teacher is always out to get you and is picking on you. A teacher is someone who may have a gun, but you are the one with the bullets. An empty gun can't hurt you, only a loaded one can. Every time you come to class unprepared, slouch in your seat, use disrespectful words, and refuse to do what you are asked, you give a bullet to the teacher. You can control whether or not you decide to give bullets to your teacher or figure out how you can keep your own bullets."

Excuses from students are unacceptable. Accept goals for better behavior, and reinforce actions that show effort in achieving those goals.

ASK A STUDENT WHO IS BEING DIFFICULT TO TEACH THE CLASS

An eye-opening and behavior-changing strategy for difficult students is to put them in the position of teaching. You might meet privately with a specific student and say, "I can't teach the class when you *(identify the behavior)*. I think you should have an opportunity to understand what it is like to prepare a lesson and teach it. Maybe I'll pick up some good ideas from you. Your turn will come tomorrow, so I thought this would be a good time for you to do some planning. The lesson will be on *(name the topic)*. If you need some help figuring things out, let me know. I'll be happy to help." Preparation for teaching the class can be the consequence for disruptive behavior. Most students become quite uncomfortable with the responsibility of teaching the class, and this often motivates them to ask for an alternative other than teaching. Better behavior while you teach can be offered as an option. You might say, "If you decide this responsibility is too much for you, I'd be happy to accept a plan for better behavior that tells me specifically what you propose to do differently so that class will not be disrupted when I teach."

HANDLING THEFT

When things turn up missing, begin by having an open-ended class discussion in which you inform the class about the missing item(s). Tell students that it makes you feel sad and upset when people take things that belong to you or to them. Ask the students if they have ever had anything of value taken from them. Allow enough time for a thorough discussion. Continue by saying, "In this classroom, people have a right to their own belongings. Nobody may take what belongs to somebody else unless they have asked for and received permission." If you suspect a specific child of the theft, make eye contact and be in close proximity to that child as you set this limit. Conclude by asking the class for suggestions about how to help the student(s) who has been stolen from. You might say, "Who has an idea about what we can do to make things right for *(name the student)*?"

Set up opportunities in class in which the child who steals can be given responsibility for doing things to combat theft. Sandi Melton, a teacher in San Antonio, Texas, tells about asking a known thief to guard her purse. She noted that there was never anything missing after she did this. Oddly, some children steal not because they want the object, but because they want what the object represents. For example, children who steal school supplies may really want to take home the teacher or classmates. Since they cannot do either, they take objects rather than people. With such children it can be helpful to actually give them some inexpensive objects from class that can be taken home (such as paper and crayons). You can also encourage the class to make gifts to one another as a way of showing their caring and generosity. Stealing is reduced when students feel nurtured. Encourage generosity through giving. If stealing persists and you have a good idea about who is doing it, refer the student to a child guidance clinic or school mental health professional for further evaluation.

DISCOURAGE EXCESSIVE TATTLING

Adults often unwittingly reinforce tattling by instructing children to tell them when they are bothered by someone else. Doing this is preferable to having the child retaliate in a harmful way. Obviously, it is better to tell than to hurt. Let your students know that dangerous, destructive, and disrespectful actions should be brought to your attention. Otherwise, teach your students that they have a right to not be bothered by others, but when they are, show them how to stand up for themselves assertively.

Habitual tattlers have failed to learn the distinction between dangerous events that warrant immediate teacher attention and those that do not. They often seek attention and approval from adults because they do not feel accepted by peers. Treat the problem as symptomatic of the child's underlying feeling of detachment from and rejection by peers. One strategy is to appreciate students when they are engaged in behaviors incompatible with tattling. For example, say, "Luis, I really like the way you are sharing your ideas with John." Privately say to Marissa, "Today you seemed to find a way to solve problems without my help. Did you notice that? How were you able to do it?" Perhaps the quickest effective strategy is to ask the tattler one of the following questions: "Is that your problem or his?" or "What do you want to do about that? Think it over, and if you want to tell me your solution, I'll be happy to listen."

Most students are entirely capable of solving their own problems when properly focused. When students show growth in their decision-making skills, it is important that we help them attribute improvement to decisions and efforts they made so that they are more likely to internalize the change. When tattling is widespread, it is advisable to do classroom role-playing in which different situations are offered that involve tattling followed by the class brainstorming alternative solutions. The solutions are listed with discussion centering on those situations in which telling the teacher is warranted (danger, destruction, disrespect) in contrast with those that can be handled in a different way (such as telling on someone who is getting a drink of water without permission). Finally, you could use the laminated ear strategy (page 61) and tell students that they can always visit the ear if they need to get stuff off their minds about each other, things going on at home, or in class. While educators need to remain open to the important issues concerning our students and be good listeners, we also want to promote independence and personal responsibility.

USE THESE THREE KEYS TO CONFRONT BULLYING: BE FIRM, CONSISTENT, AND LOW KEY

There has rightfully been considerable attention focused on the issue of bullying in recent years. Formal, structured programs have been developed to help schools handle this problem effectively. Although bullying is a complex issue that involves understanding the dynamics of those who bully along with those who are victimized, all students have a right to feel safe from the abuse of others. We can best contribute to school safety by confronting inappropriate comments and behaviors that we see and hear *firmly, consistently,* and in a *low-key* manner.

There should be a respectful but no-nonsense approach. Matter-of-fact comments delivered in a friendly yet certain manner such as "We don't do that here," "That language doesn't belong here," and "That was disrespectful" are usually sufficient. It is best to convey these comments with as much privacy, eye contact, and close proximity as possible (P.E.P., page 94), although when the bullying is openly apparent to others, public confrontation is appropriate. When students know that adults will act assertively, they feel safer. Finally, improved behavior can actually be expedited by thanking the student for his or her compliance before it is received. A simple follow-up comment to those involved—such as "Thanks for your cooperation"—often works wonders.

HANDLING GROUP MISBEHAVIOR

For preventing group misbehavior, it is wise to invite students to join you in developing classroom rules. Most teachers find that when students are more invested in the rules because they have had a hand in developing them, they tend to behave better and are more likely to confront each other when misbehavior occurs. Other tips in this book provide guidance. In addition, the following strategies can help you manage difficult group behavior. The strategies you select will depend upon the dynamics of your classroom and your style of intervention:

- Meet with the class ringleaders at a separate time to acknowledge their leadership. You might say something like, "Most days, I notice too little teaching and learning in our class because of *(name the problems, such as interruptions, fights, name-calling, and so on)*. I am tired of lecturing, yelling, and threatening. While I am prepared to continue doing this or whatever else it may take to have our class run smoothly, I hope you can offer some ideas about how our class can work better together. How are we going to fix this problem?" If the ringleaders protest and complain that you are picking on them, say, "I know you are not the only one(s) breaking the rule, but you are the classroom leaders. It is clear that others look to you for approval. So how are we going to fix this problem?" When several students are misbehaving, it is usually more efficient and effective to meet with the leaders for problem-solving rather than trying to get everyone on board. Ringleaders are more motivated to influence change when their thoughts and opinions are valued.

- Provide consequences to the least powerful "groupie," and gradually work your way up. Students who are followers are unlikely to battle with you. Your real purpose is to send an indirect message to the leaders that you do not accept inappropriate behavior, and you will take action if it continues. When possible, you do not want to back strong oppositional students into a corner because power struggles almost always result.

- Allow students to develop a "reward cookbook" of activities and privileges they enjoy. Keep a daily record of classroom disruptions and tell the students that on each day (or week) improvement is observed, they can choose one of the activities during a designated time. Instead of doing this with all students, a related option would be to establish this system with the few who are particularly adept at orchestrating the unacceptable behavior. Improvement shown by them leads to the entire class earning a reward. Since ringleaders are generally seeking power and influence, they are essentially given the power to influence whether or not the class earns extra privileges or rewards.

Another possibility is to have your students decide whether or not their behavior warranted a reward. It generally works best to make this a "job" of responsibility within the class. You can have a small subgroup of students make this decision (on a rotating basis), including the students who are most challenging. We have found that when students are given this level of responsibility, they are usually quite accurate in determining whether or not the behavior has been achieved.

- Advise students to use the suggestion box, as mentioned on page 73, and solicit ideas from the class that they believe will solve the problem.

- Try to interact with ringleaders informally at other times of the school day. You might find your way to their lunch table, and while eating together, you can bring up your concerns about the class. You can use this time to seek suggestions about how to make the class a better place for everyone.

- If an obvious behavior problem occurs during class and you do not see it happen, an effective guideline is to assume that everyone in the classroom did it. For example, if your back is turned and somebody throws something, hold the entire class accountable. Do not argue or raise your voice. Simply say, "I am not going to get into a hassle about this. It is our classroom, and we are all responsible for what goes on here. Let's pick it up." For certain behaviors, you might even have a *reparations squad* whose job is to handle things such as messy floors and misaligned desks. The squad can be assigned or selected on a rotating basis or by drawing straws.

AUDIO- OR VIDEOTAPING THE CLASS

When problems are occurring and full awareness of the situation is lacking, tape your class. Due to issues of privacy, it is best to define the purpose of the taping as an opportunity for you, the teacher, to learn how to be better at behavior management. Tell this to your students, and be sure to receive permission from the administration before proceeding. While taping, try to focus on those students who give you the most difficulty. After class, when you have captured an incident or series of disruptions, meet with the students who are causing the problems. Show them or let them listen to the tape, and discuss your feelings and theirs about the way they looked or sounded. Ask them what they would do if they were the teacher. When given a chance to actually see or hear themselves, students often gain an awareness of their negative impact and are willing to try something new. To help make this procedure more effective, let them know that since you will now be making some changes based upon their suggestions, you will want to tape again to decide if their strategy worked. Expressing a spirit of openness in our willingness to be a part of the taping—so that students can help us fix "our" problem—can go a long way towards gaining their cooperation and commitment to change. Your suggestions and your students' suggestions regarding change should be specific and manageable.

Use of taping can also be extremely helpful when you wish to provide evidence or give direct feedback to others with whom you work who are also connected to the child. For example, the parents of a child who is disruptive or troubled may become more motivated to seek outside support if they see their child's problems in the classroom context. It is one thing to hear about problems from somebody and quite another to actually see or listen to the behavior.

Be sure to get necessary permission from administration and perhaps parents to do classroom taping. Permission is easier to get when you define the specific purpose for taping along with the benefits that are likely to be gained. For example, tell parents, "I'd like to get your permission to set up a videotape so that you can witness for yourself how your child is doing. I know that we both want your child to be successful, and I find that many children and their parents are much better able to appreciate how things are going when they get to see their children in action. Further, it helps me evaluate my classroom so that improvements can be made when necessary. Your cooperation is appreciated."

TRAFFIC SCHOOL

John W. Cochol, a principal at an alternative secondary school in New York, wrote the following letter describing the benefits of an approach to correcting student behavior developed by staff following training in Discipline With Dignity. Mr. Cochol writes:

> The **Traffic School** was born out of a need to get away from the constant power struggles that can occur at bus arrival and departure times. It is a frustrating time, and there were a variety of safety concerns. Staff was getting more punitive (such as taking away tokens or points already earned, carryover time outs, or in-school suspension) while actually looking for and trying more positive interventions. Following a conference at which you shared your information, I suggested we try a new way that would focus on teaching or remediation of the behaviors we expected during these times. Students are issued traffic tickets by staff with a duplicate going to the office. At the start of our preferred activity period (earned activities the last 25 minutes of the day), students with traffic violations attend *traffic class* for 10 minutes. The staff assigns, instructs, and has students practice safe and appropriate hallway or bus behaviors corresponding with the violations noted. Some students will write or draw about the infraction and the corresponding safety rules. When they

are done, the students attend the preferred activity already in progress.

In the beginning many students thought this technique was a joke, and there were many repeat violators. We are now going into our fourth year with super success. Each year the numbers have decreased along with the opportunity for power struggles. There are still repeat offenders, and staff has been using some "community service" opportunities as an extension to the class. We have also added positive recognition at our annual awards assembly for students who do not receive violations.

HANDLING STUDENTS WHO ARE TURNED OFF AND HAVE SHUT DOWN

Students who shut down are extremely hard to engage because they usually do not want to experience anew the pain they have previously experienced through failure and rejection. Most will manifest a shut-down mannerism by not working and having an "I don't care" attitude. It is important to realize that these students did not begin life or school unmotivated. People learn to become unmotivated when they are continually put in situations exceeding their capacity and without proper support. Look at each turned-off student as a person trying to protect him- or herself from the fear of failure. When we give up, the first thing that goes is our attitude. Reawakening an "I can do it" belief system and the energy required for school success necessitates a great deal of trust, which is not easily gained. We must maintain and communicate a "can do" attitude fueled by a refusal to give up on kids when they are giving up on themselves. The following tips can help you help these students.

Make a daily commitment to extend friendly interaction with each turned-off student. Demonstrate an interest in his or her current pursuits and activities, no matter how mundane the circumstances.

*Every time you hear a student say, "I don't care," "I don't know,"
or "I can't," add the word "yet."* This conveys your belief that mastery is just a matter of time and effort rather than a fixed feature that cannot be changed. Consider phrases like these as expressions of fear. "I don't care" virtually always means, "I'm afraid that if I did care I wouldn't measure up anyway, so why care or try?" You might post defeatist phrases, such as the one above, in the classroom and write the word "yet" after each in big bold letters.

Challenge the failure attitude forcefully yet respectfully. When you hear or see a defeatist attitude, let that student know that you understand the required work has probably been difficult to do in the past. Assure the student that not all of us are good at everything. There are no guarantees those things we are not good at will ever become easy. Further, let these students know that you will not give up on them today, tomorrow, or ever, and express your deeper concern when it looks as if these students have already given up on themselves. Actual words may sound something like, "Rachel, I know so far this is not your most interesting subject nor is it likely what you do best. Nobody likes to work hard when success does not come easily, but I have no doubt that you will get much better at this by putting forth more effort. It may never become your best area, but you will get better. Even if you keep giving up on yourself, I will never show you disrespect by giving up on you. It takes courage to fight the feeling of failure and to keep at what you are trying to achieve. But I know you are tough. Now let's get going."

Try to avoid giving assignments that are overwhelming. When kids care about learning and succeeding, they feel anxious when they are required to do things that they do not know. If the anxiety does not give way to eventual mastery, then students will protect themselves by not caring about the work. It becomes too scary with too much anxiety to put forth effort without results. Identify effort parameters for your students. For example, tell them that 15 minutes is the most you want them spending on any math problem. If they have not figured it out by then, there is no shame. Offer choices such as calling the homework hotline, asking a math helper friend for advice, or advising them to try to do as much work as they can on the problems, but bring in the rest during the next class meeting for assistance.

Tips for Helping Students Handle Tough Moments and Difficult Situations

8

Strong people make as many ugly mistakes as weak people. The difference is that strong people admit them, laugh at them, and learn from them. That is how they become strong.

—Richard Needham, Author and Educator

This section offers strategies we can teach our students—some are designed to help them stand up to others when their buttons are pushed, while other strategies emphasize learning ways of maintaining self-control.

SIX STEPS IN TEACHING ALTERNATIVES TO HURTING OTHERS

Students who repeatedly say or do hurtful things are often hurting inside. They learn to hurt others first, before others hurt them, as a form of self-protection. Although many such students need ongoing interventions to help them get a handle on things (ideally, in concert with their families), educators can benefit these students and all others affected through an ongoing six-step process. We need to ask ourselves how we want our students to express anger with us. When they do not like something that you say or do, how do you want them to let you know? Should they tell you? How? What words should they use, and when should they tell you? Is it okay with you if they tell you right away (even if you are in the middle of a lesson), or are there certain times set aside for you to listen? Do you want them to write how they feel? What if they are too young to write or if they hate writing? Are there other alternatives? Can they draw a picture of how upset they are? Should they tell a friend first and get some advice before coming to you?

Your answers to these questions can provide you with strategies for teaching your students. Once you are clear about these expectations, the first step is to *model* how you want your students to express themselves towards you. You might even model a session in which one of your students becomes angry at you so that you can show all of your students how you want them to react when someone makes them angry. The next step is to *teach* the specific skills that you want to see. Not all of your students may have the skills to do what you ask of them, and some will need *practice.* Setting up role-playing situations can be a helpful way to provide practice for your students. Even after they possess the skills you want to teach them, it will be important for you and them to *evaluate* how these skills are working. Are you noticing improvement? Are they? For areas that are not improving, it will be necessary to *re-teach* the skills or *explore other options.* In summary, the six steps in teaching alternatives to hurting others are:

1. Model behavior.
2. Teach skills.
3. Practice skills.
4. Evaluate effectiveness.
5. Re-teach when necessary.
6. Find other options.

TEACH "REAL" STANDING UP FOR YOURSELF

Impulsive students who are quick to lose control need to learn to ask themselves two primary questions as soon as they become angry:

1. Who is pushing my buttons?

2. Am I going to let him or her win?

When endeavoring to teach students better self-control, start by asking them all the things they can think of that other people say or do that make them mad. List all of the specifics they share with you, and then ask, "When others say or do these things, do you think they are trying to give you power or rob you of your power?" With younger students, simplify the question by asking them if hearing these things from others makes them feel strong or weak. With very young children, ask them if they think others are trying to make them feel very happy or very sad. Ask them who wins if they let others make them feel weak or sad, or get them into trouble.

Use this process to lead into the teaching of strategies in which students can stand up for themselves without giving their power away. Some strategies may be very obvious but need to be reviewed because they are typically always offered, but often ineffective. For example, adults usually suggest *ignoring* and *moving away* as the primary strategies for students to use when someone says or does something they find offensive. While these age-old ideas still have value, many students are concerned about looking like a wimp, thereby inviting further abuse if they move away. A strategy has to fit the student's temperament and personality, so there is no single way to handle all of these situations. For many, ignoring and moving away can work well. You might even ask students to identify times in which they either ignored or walked away from a situation and it worked. Suggest that they continue to ignore or move away when others are bugging them because it is simple to remember and easy to do. At the same time, we need to teach students more assertive ways to handle these moments.

We can help the more aggressive students by complimenting them on their desire to stand up for themselves and then exploring assertive strategies that they can use which will not get them into trouble. Use words such as, "I have noticed that when you get picked on, you don't just sit back and take it. It is good to stand up for yourself and show others that they can't push you around. But fighting, pushing, or calling names is against the rules. If you do those things, you will always get into trouble. Would you like to hear about some other ways that you can stand up for yourself *without* getting into trouble?" It can also help to pose questions such as:

- Is Luis trying to give you power or rob you of your power when he pushes your buttons?

- If he robs you of your power by getting you into trouble, then who wins?

- Do you want to give him what he wants?

- Are you interested in learning other things you might say or do to keep your own power the next time you are faced with this kind of situation?

When students are motivated, share your own ideas and strategies you currently use, or apply suggestions and techniques from this book. If you are unsure about how you might best handle a situation faced by a student, you might say, "I'm not exactly sure what I would do, but which students in our class seem able to stand up for themselves and gain the respect they are looking for? What do they say or do? Which of these strategies might you want to borrow?"

VARIATIONS ON I-MESSAGES

Expressing feelings through I-messages has been taught to students for a long time. An I-message is an assertive way for a person to stand up for him- or herself without attacking back. A traditional I-message has three parts:

1. Tell someone what bothers you.

2. Tell how you feel.

3. Express what you want.

Here are two examples:

1. "When you were talking about me to the other girls,
2. I felt mad and left out.
3. I want you to stop doing that."

1. "When you called me a fat slob and told me to get out of your face,
2. it made me feel sad and mad.
3. I don't call you names, and I don't want to be called hurtful

The traditional I-message script includes three steps:

1. When _____ *(describe what bothers you),*

2. I feel *(become or get)* _____ *(describe how what is troubling you makes you feel).*

3. So what I want *(or need or expect)* from you is _____ *(describe what must take place to resolve the situation).*

Consider this example of an educator using an I-message while confronting a difficult student:

> *When* you blow me off and leave the building or office, *I feel* like we have failed you and are not meeting your needs because there is something wrong here that we haven't fixed or haven't addressed. *What I need* is for you to sit in the outer office and think about what caused the problem and tell me how we should fix it.

Tell them how you feel and make a deal. After teaching I-messages, encourage your students to compromise. Here are several examples:

- "When you took my chicken fingers *(tell what happened)*, I felt mad *(tell how you feel)*, so I've decided that unless you give them back or buy me new ones, I'm not playing with you at recess *(make a deal)*."

- "When you call me names *(tell what happened)*, I have no interest in hanging out with you *(how you feel)*, and so I'm just going my own way unless you act in a more decent way *(make a deal)*."

Bug/Want. This variation works especially well with younger children. They are simply taught to say what bugs them and what they want. For example, "It *bugs* me when you cut in line. I *want* you to wait your turn."

NO HITTING BELOW THE BELT

Use the image of getting hit above or below the belt when confronting hurtful or bullying behavior. Educators agree that hurtful actions and language must be effectively confronted for a safe learning environment to exist. One very effective way to convey this to students is to have them identify all of the things that they hear or see at school that are painful. Ask them, "What are some things you see or hear inside or outside the classroom that would make you angry if somebody said or did these things to you?" Invariably, students will list a multitude of things. The next step is to ask if anyone has ever been hit, even accidentally, "below the belt," where it really hurts. This question will usually evoke a groan among middle-school and high-school students. Explain that when people say or do hurtful things to each other, it is like hitting someone below the belt. In boxing, above the belt is allowed, but below the belt is a foul. Ask, "Why do you think those are the rules? What do you think you might eventually do if you keep getting hit over and over below the belt?" Most answers fall into two categories: withdraw or strike back.

Explain that when people expect to be hurt, they will usually protect themselves by putting up a wall. If this happens enough and a person is in constant pain, then he or she may want to end the pain. Some students hurt themselves as a way of ending the pain. Other students get angry and "hit back," sometimes in a violent way. That can create danger for others. You might ask, "If someone kept punching you, what would you do?" Conclude by telling them that it would be wise and safe to avoid hitting below the belt and to treat each other in a way that makes sure that the school remains a safe place.

After presenting this concept, you can remind students of it when they are in conflict. For example, when you see students being mean to each other, you can confront the attacking student by saying, "Was that above the belt or below? Raise those fists."

USE SELF-MONITORING METHODS TO TEACH SELF-CONTROL

When students lack awareness of what they are doing or they seem unable to monitor their own behavior, help is warranted through a variety of behavior modification methods. Traditional behavior modification has the teacher offering different valued rewards for achievement of a desirable behavior. Charts are often used to monitor performance. If students achieve sufficient behavior control, then they receive the reward. Although the traditional method is needed for students who are cognitively limited or excessively neurologically driven, many students can benefit from self-monitoring programs in which they are put in charge of watching their own behavior, with rewards being given only if they cannot sustain more positive behavior without the reward. Examples of self-monitoring charts appear on page 132. Instructions for using the charts begin on page 133.

OOPS!

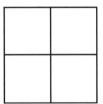

I DID IT!

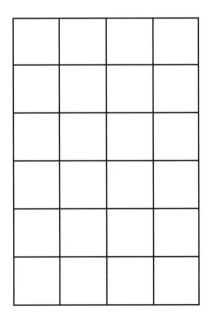

1. Meet with the student with excessive behavior (for example, out of his or her seat, calling out, interrupting, and asking endless questions).

2. Tell the student, "I made a little gift for you that I think is going to help you stay in your seat better *(name actual behavior)* because we both know that sitting is difficult for you. Would you like to see my gift?" *(Give the chart to the student, preferably with the student's name on it.)*

3. Then say, "Let me show you how it works: On the left side where it says, 'I did it!' there are boxes underneath. Do you see those? Good. During reading group today, when you feel like getting out of your seat but don't because you remind yourself that it is against the rules, I want you to put a star or sticker in one of these boxes. Which would you like?" After the student decides, explain, "'I did it!' means that you remembered to follow the rules without anyone having to remind you."

4. Finally, explain, "On the right side are boxes under where you see 'Oops!' If you make a mistake and get out of your seat when you aren't supposed to, just as soon as you think 'Oops, I'm supposed to be back in my seat,' and then you go back to your seat without being reminded, I want you to put a check mark in one of those boxes. Which side do you think is going to have more boxes filled during reading group today?" Most kids want to fill up the bigger side with stickers.

For most students, this is sufficient, and nothing more involved is needed. For some, a preferred activity that is specific and concrete can be earned to reinforce improvement.

Another successful technique used to teach self-control is to give a student a certain number of 2×2 paper squares. The exact number given to the student depends upon how often a certain behavior occurs. For example, if a student calls out continuously during the day, it might be necessary to give him or her 10 squares. Say that each time the student calls out without raising a hand to be recognized, he or she has to pay one square. When there are no more squares, the student is no longer allowed to call out. This is sufficient to get most students to monitor their own behavior. Some may need a more tangible reward that can be predetermined. For example, extra playtime or selection of a preferred activity can be earned for each square that has not been spent at the end of the day (morning or afternoon period might be a more appropriate time interval).

USE ACRONYMS TO TEACH STUDENTS ACCEPTABLE BEHAVIOR

Acronyms are great ways to help students easily remember certain tips or techniques associated with proper behavior. For example, after discussing rules and consequences, you can let your students know that they are to use the "triple D" guideline when deciding about whether to tell an adult about somebody else's behavior. The three Ds stand for *dangerous, destructive,* and *disrespectful.* We should be encouraging students to handle issues as independently as possible in order to build responsibility, but when they see or experience someone doing something that falls into the category of one of the three Ds, then they should tell us. A list of helpful acronyms appears on the next page.

Helpful Acronyms

TAG (to be used when someone does something you do not like)
   Tell someone what he or she is doing that bothers you.
   Ask them to stop.
   Go tell someone.

STOMP (to be used when angry)
   Stop before you do anything (take a breath).
   Think about what happened and what you want to do.
   Options (what are the consequences of each choice?).
   Move on it (make a choice).
   Praise yourself (for not losing control and doing your best).

Q-TIP (to help to not take bad things personally)
   Quit
   Taking
   It
   Personally

STAR (to be used as a problem-solving device)
   Stop.
   Think about your options.
   Act (make a choice).
   Review (how did it go?).

ICCM (to promote self-control)
   I
   Can
   Control
   Myself

RESPECT
   I will:
   Respect others and myself.
   Exhibit self-control.
   Succeed!
   Participate.
   Encourage!
   Cooperate.
   Try!

WINNERS (taught by Chris Coppelli)
   What is the problem?
   Identify possible solutions.
   Narrow it down to the best choice.
   Now do it.
   Every action counts.
   React peacefully.
   Stick with it.

USE COUPONS THAT ALLOW FOR LIMITED RULE-BREAKING

An unconventional way to establish order around inappropriate behavior (especially when the behavior occurs frequently) is to legitimize it. Paradoxically, when someone who often acts in a defiant way is encouraged to do the thing they do automatically, they actually start doing it less often. Yes, that is correct: As crazy as it sounds, you can actually achieve better behavior by allowing and even encouraging a limited amount of inappropriate behavior.

Our book *Discipline With Dignity* (Curwin & Mendler, 1988, 1999) gives several examples of how to change behavior by acting in a paradoxical way. Essentially, you encourage the opposite of what you really want. You can create a variation of paradoxical interventions by creating coupons that encourage a limited amount of the very behavior that you want to stop. Start by making a list of all the things that your students do that you find objectionable—such as sleeping in class, speaking out of turn, drumming on desks, and leaving seats without permission. Next, cross out all the aggressive behaviors (hitting, kicking, biting, and bullying others). With the remaining items on your list (those that are disruptive but not harmful), consider making a booklet of permission coupons that entitle the holder to perform the behavior described on the coupon. Students are then required to give you that coupon when they want to do the behavior. They may do the behavior as long as they have a coupon.

You can use this method with individual students who excessively act inappropriately, or apply it to an entire class. You will need to decide how many coupons would be adequate for a given behavior. For example, a high-school teacher effectively managed requests to use the bathroom by giving each student three bathroom passes and telling them that the passes were good for the entire semester. As long as students had a coupon and wanted to use it, they could. Students understood that if they did not possess a coupon, then they could not leave the room except under extraordinary circumstances. The following list describes some of the behaviors that could be addressed with coupons.

Coupon Behaviors

- Being late to class
- Talking out of turn
- Saying goofy or silly things
- Getting out of one's seat and cruising around the classroom
- Going to the bathroom
- Going to the nurse's office
- Using curse words
- Not listening in class
- Not getting in line
- Tapping objects on the desk
- Complaining that it is too hard or saying, "I can't" or "I'm unable"
- Asking, "When will I ever use this?"
- Asking, "Will this be on the test?"
- Saying, "This is stupid."
- Making an excuse
- Losing or forgetting your homework
- Saying something that you know will be irritating
- Clowning around
- Telling a lie
- Entertaining the class with a joke
- Singing a song or performing a dance
- Talking loud
- Forgetting your books
- Getting out of your seat 1 minute before the bell rings

When doing this with an individual or a small group of students, it is best to determine the number of coupons in collaboration with them during a private meeting. For example, say, "Paula, I hate bugging you all the time about speaking out of turn. You have a lot to say and I understand that it is not always easy to wait. But I need to hear from other students, too. So how many times do you think you will need to speak out of turn today? A few times is okay." If the student comes up with a number that is excessive, say so: "Paula, that is too many. I know I'd be frustrated, and we'd probably get into another power struggle. I can live with between _____ and _____ (*name a narrow range that you could live with*). Pick an amount that might be hard for you to handle but you think you could." Then give the student that many coupons.

In addition, you could have some of your coupons specify a time interval, for example, 1 minute of pencil tapping or a 5-minute trip to the bathroom. Design your coupons with a personal touch (such as your name or image on the coupon). If you lack artistic skill, have some of your students or an art class design and print the coupons that suit your needs.

"KISS UP" RESPONSES THAT ADULTS LIKE TO HEAR

Teach your students how to respond in a positive way to adults. Many students who frequently get into trouble do little to endear themselves to teachers and administrators. We can teach them that using certain words and phrases regularly will help them make a positive impression so that they are less likely to get into trouble. Some of my favorites I like to teach students are:

- Yes.
- Okay.
- I didn't mean it.
- I'm sorry.
- It will never happen again.
- May I please?
- I'll give it a try.
- Excuse me.
- When you get a moment, could you . . .
- Good morning.
- Thanks for your help.
- That was a good lesson.

THE CONFUSION TECHNIQUE

Pat Curran, dean of students at Calvert Hall High School in Baltimore, runs detention at his school. He starts detention by going over expected behavior and then introduces his "confusion policy." In Pat's words, the technique is as follows:

> Please don't confuse me with your behavior. For example, if your eyes are closed and your head is on the desk, I will probably think you are sleeping, which is against the

rules. So if you are not really asleep, do not confuse me into thinking that you are, because I won't really know if you are sleeping or not. Therefore, please do not confuse me and cause me to make a mistake by giving you another day of detention.

Pat presents this policy in a joking manner. Afterwards, all he usually has to do when a student is breaking the rule is say, "Denny, you know you are confusing me," and the student will smile and try to stay awake and keep his eyes open. Pat does the same thing with other behaviors such as talking: "If you are looking at someone, smiling, or moving your lips, you'll confuse me into thinking you are talking."

part 4

Tips for Specific Problems and Circumstances— Questions and Answers

9 Questions and Answers

Tell me and I may forget. Show me and I may remember.
Involve me and I'll understand.

—Chinese Proverb

Situation

I have a student in my first-grade class who talks all the time. He has a comment about everything and answers for everyone. His mother told me that this is not a new problem. The preacher at their church purposefully asks the child for his opinion at an early point in the sermon, hopefully so the child will feel somewhat less obligated to keep interrupting as the sermon continues. It is beyond annoying.

Analysis/Solution

This is probably a highly anxious child who deep down is concerned that he does not matter unless he hears himself speak. I think the preacher is on the right track. Ask for the child's opinion early in the day and then again at later intervals. Tell the child that you are very interested in hearing him talk (identify the specific times you will listen to him), but explain that being quiet and keeping thoughts inside until it is time to talk is a sign of growing up. Ask him to watch the behavior of adults in places such as the cafeteria to see what he notices about how often they speak. You might arrange to have him spend some time with older students while asking him to keep score on how many times each student talks. Perhaps it would be possible to give him a job in the classroom that requires him to be the person who makes sure that everyone gets a chance to be heard when questions are asked. Give him a class roster and tell him, "When I ask the class a question, and it is not your turn to answer, I want you to put a circle around the name of the person that I call on to give an answer. I will check with you a few times each day to make sure that everyone gets a chance to speak."

Situation

I have a child who must always be the center of attention. If she is not the first one called on for everything, she runs around the room, sings, taps pencils, and pokes other students. When I attempt to discuss behavior with her, she shakes her head back and forth, sings, and clicks her tongue or spins.

Analysis/Solution

It would be wise to have this child evaluated for the possibility of Attention Deficit Hyperactivity Disorder (ADHD). The behaviors you describe are often associated with this condition, and she may respond well to a trial of medication. You might explore developing a behavior modification program in which specific categories such as waiting one's turn, following rules, and getting along with others are charted, with the child being evaluated during various intervals of the day as to how well she has done. Points can be earned for proper behavior and traded for specific predetermined privileges. It is often helpful to get parents on board as it may sometimes be more practical for the child to earn the privileges at home based upon school performance. Finally, you might work to help the child learn to share attention with others. For example, call on her and another student simultaneously to answer a question, or ask her to run an errand with another student. Try having her work in a small group while assigning roles to each child. Be sure to give her times when her job is important and she receives attention, such as when she is the group reporter, and other times when her job is also important but she receives less attention, such as when she is the time-keeper. You might also ask her to be a question-asking helper. Tell her that you will be calling on other children to answer questions about the story that was just read, and you want to make sure that each child feels confident that he or she knows what the story was about. Her job is to check with each of these children by asking them if they are ready to answer the question. If they say they are, then she is to move on. If they are not sure, then she can be their helper by assisting them while they get prepared. You could also consider using coupons (see page 138) and/or colored paper clips (see page 62).

Situation

I have a bunch of kids who do not care about any of the consequences. More and more, I encounter stubbornness with students who say, "I don't want to," or "No, I'm not going to," or they just drop out of the activity altogether. They refuse to work and often encourage each other's misbehavior. Some become hostile and offensive when I speak to them, which launches profanity outbursts and verbal harassment. What should I do?

Analysis/Solution

You will find the tips on handling group misbehavior (pages 116–118) and responses to oppositional behavior (pages 96–99) to be quite useful. Rely more on gaining your students' respect than on discovering effective consequences. Translate their words "I don't want to" to mean "I'm afraid to try because I might fail, and then I'd feel bad." Tell them that learning can sometimes be hard and does not always lead to success right away. Give yourself permission to make mistakes in their presence and then work though the process, showing them that no one is perfect. When you see or hear inappropriate behavior directed at you, confront it in a firm way. For example, you could say, "I feel disrespected. Is that what you meant? I don't listen when such words are hurled in my direction. We both know that there is a better way, and you will use respectful language if you are serious about getting my attention to listen to your complaints." Another option is to firmly confront one or more of the leaders by saying, "Bill, it looks like you are trying to embarrass me in front of everyone, and that only makes me feel like embarrassing you back. We both know that beginning right now there are more respectful ways you can use to be noticed. Your cooperation is appreciated."

One very effective strategy is to meet and confront the stronger opinion makers for problem-solving at a separate time. You can use many of the tips for problem-solving in this book to involve these student leaders in solving the problem. To begin, you might say, "When _____ *(identify the problem)* happens, a dilemma is created because I can't teach and, more importantly, students can't learn. Others in the class think of you as the leaders, so together we will have to fix this problem. I would prefer that we handle this together, so I can stop nagging, bugging, and giving consequences. Who has some ideas?"

Situation

A discipline scenario that I always find challenging is the defiant kid who refuses to comply with a request to remove him- or herself from a classroom where he or she has been a disturbance. This refusal to leave the room makes the event even more disturbing.

Analysis/Solution

You describe a typical power struggle sequence characterized by continued escalation. Recognize that it always takes two for a power struggle to occur. Most power struggles can be handled by use of P.E.P. (see page 94). Try a supportive attitude toward the student who is unwilling to leave the classroom. For example, "Tiffany, I know you are not happy right now, and probably you have a lot to say to me that is important for me to hear. I can and will listen to you later. This is not the time." As an educator, always strive to avoid having to ask students to leave the classroom, but also make it difficult for students to continue their misbehavior. Expecting compliance without choices from an oppositional student just does not happen. Be sure to give a choice even when you are at the point of ordering the student out of the classroom. For example: "Kim, you and I both know your behavior is unacceptable. Either get back to doing the right thing, or you will need to leave the class. I hope you decide to stay." Finally, recognize that students who chronically escalate their behavior are usually seeking a sense of power and influence. Look for opportunities to empower these students by recognizing them, giving them high status things to do in the classroom, or by simply asking for their opinions from time to time.

Situation

I have a difficult time getting and maintaining the attention of my students during a lesson. Many tap, talk, space out, have a lack of focus, and fall off their chairs. I feel like I have tried everything with little or no success.

Analysis/Solution

About once every 7 years, even the best teachers will be given a class that is a struggle from day one. Unfortunately, there is no simple solution to fixing all of these problems, but there are several things that can be done to improve most situations. You might step back and try to assess your students' interests, abilities, and needs. Consider giving an interest inventory to each student, and carefully consider their responses. Their answers can lead to ideas about how you might modify things for better results. Another option is to meet with small focus groups within the class and ask them to identify their likes and dislikes. Ask them to respond to prompts such as:

- "I wish in school we could do more _____."
  (Ask the students what they would like to do more often.)

- "I learn best when _____." *(Ask your students what offers them optimum learning conditions.)*

- "I think we could all concentrate better in class if _____."
  (Ask them to describe or list some of the things that they find distracting.)

Most teachers report that rules tend to be followed better when students play an active role in the development and modification of the rules. At an early point in the school year, invite them to join in making the classroom a better place. You might say, "Too many rules are being broken in our class. Let's look at what you think I need to do and what you think you need to do that will make our class work better." Finally, it might be wise to consult a trusted and admired colleague for input and a sympathetic ear when you need to share your concerns and frustrations. Invite your associate to observe your class; his or her objectivity may bring a fresh approach to the problems. Your colleague may be able to see and identify some things that you cannot see. This colleague may share ideas and techniques that will lead to better behavior and more learning in your classroom. You can sometimes also get ideas for improving student behavior by visiting the classroom of an admired colleague to see how he or she establishes order.

Situation

I have a child who will flare up with a tantrum because he thinks someone looked at him funny. While in a tantrum, he'll throw chairs or run away. Despite many efforts at planning and working with him in which he can tell me what he will do differently "the next time," there

are times when he explodes with anger. After the explosion settles down, everything is fine. In the meantime, other children are in danger due to this one child's problem behavior.

Analysis/Solution

It sounds like this child may have juvenile bipolar disorder, which is often characterized by rapidly fluctuating wide mood-swings including agitation, depression, and explosive behavior. For this child it would be wise to recommend a thorough medical work-up along with a psychological assessment conducted by a professional familiar with this disorder. It is also not unusual for these students to have a co-occurrence of ADHD and learning problems. Medication along with behavioral intervention can often help the student feel better, resulting in less agitation.

The student will need help learning to recognize when he is experiencing a heightened level of emotional arousal because this usually precedes explosive behavior. Some children learn to identify their own physiological changes such as rapid breathing, a sensation of heat around the face, and increased motor activity. Others learn to identify within themselves feelings of disappointment, sadness, and anger. Occasionally a child might be able to give a name to the thoughts, feelings, and sensations that overwhelm him and can identify things in the environment that act as triggers for explosiveness, such as being told to follow a rule or being bossed around by another child. The goal is for the child to learn how to identify the triggers and then learn effective strategies for coping.

Often, school counselors have been taught ways to teach these coping strategies and are an excellent resource. Management strategies for addressing this behavior can include simple things such as learning to take a few deep breaths or count to 10. It is wise to identify a specific location in the room or school where the student can go when loss of control becomes an issue. If a location outside the classroom is identified as the designated place, be careful to monitor and keep in mind that some students will be tempted to use this safe place as a way to avoid all difficult or demanding situations. In this situation, behavior modification methods can be useful. For example, the student may be allowed to earn extra privileges for tantrum-free days. The exact system will depend upon the child's current behavior. Finally, some students do well when they know that they can have a limited number of tantrums. If your explosive student averages five episodes each week, you might give the student four "passes" at the beginning of the first week, requiring the student to trade a pass for a tantrum. It is wise to identify an acceptable location for the tantrum as well. Any passes that remain at the end of the week can be traded for a reward that includes the whole class. In this way, classmates have an incentive to provide support for their troubled classmate.

Keep in mind that explosive student behavior can be scary and upsetting to everyone. The tips in this book for handling crisis situations provide a framework that can minimize the impact of this very troubling behavior.

Situation

One student continuously refuses to do her work. How do I interest her and not give her extra reward for the work she is supposed to do?

Analysis/Solution

To keep students interested, make your curriculum relevant to her abilities and interests. As mentioned throughout this book, students are not unmotivated from birth: They learn to shut down when one or more of their basic needs are not met. Usually, there is a problem with the basic need for competence and/or power that motivates refusals. The longer-term solution is therefore to set this student up for success (make it difficult for her to fail) and find positive ways within the classroom for her to influence what goes on.

Your question implies that you use rewards to motivate interest and you are concerned that she will either hold you hostage for a reward or that other students will think it is unfair for her to get a special reward while they are not rewarded for doing the same things. Although you can handle this concern through implementation of a classroom policy to be fair and not necessarily treat all students the same, you can also have the troubling student's compliance earn a reward for the entire class. In this way, everyone gets rewarded with something extra for her effort and compliance.

Situation

I have a student who always has to be on the winning end of every situation. He is forever doing or not doing the opposite of what I ask. I don't know what to do.

Analysis/Solution

Begin by assuming that this student's need for power and influence is very intense. Many conventional strategies can start to turn things around, such as asking for his opinion, giving him responsibility by putting him in charge of selected activities, doing problem-solving, involving him in the rule-making process, and even getting him to participate in school decision-making committees that look for student input. It is very important that you remove yourself emotionally from his decisions. You need to care about him without caring too much about the choices he makes.

Try to avoid yes or no situations by being sure to provide choices. A friend of mine who now has grown children tells about a seminar on parenting that she attended when her children were very young. She said that the instructor made the point that a 2 year old always wants to run outside and could care less about taking the time to put on a coat while her parent always wants to make sure she wears a coat before going outside. The instructor suggested that the parent bring the coat to the youngster and ask, "Which sleeve do you want to put on first?" My friend relates that this lesson stayed with her and guided her throughout her child's developmental years—she was now giving the child *choices*. Give the disturbing child limited but clear choices. For example:

- Would you prefer to do your work now or during recess?

- You can write down your answer, tell me in person, or record it on tape. Which do you think would be best for you?

An unconventional method that can often be effective when students are extremely oppositional is to encourage them to keep doing exactly the opposite of what you really want them to do. Since the issue is power, many students do not want to surrender control to an adult by doing what is asked of them. Tell the student:

> Terry, I cannot make you do your assignment. I have already tried everything I know. So from now on I will completely respect your decisions. Beginning today, you will have no homework. If you come late, I will appreciate that you took the trouble to show up at all. You will get a zero as always if you do not do your homework, and I will submit a referral, as I am required when you come late, but I will no longer hassle you about it. You deserve to be respected, and I will honor that. It is about time that I appreciate you for who you are without trying to change you.

Many students are shocked at first and continue to do the very behaviors you want to change. Eventually, most realize that their oppositional behavior no longer pays off, and they actually begin to act in a more compliant way. Before you do this type of intervention, however, it is wise to clear it with your school administrator as well as parents, if they are accessible, or those responsible for the child.

Situation

When I am teaching class and explaining new content, students in my class have a hard time being quiet and staying on task. My students sit in pairs at tables. Getting them to stop talking with their neighbor is the most difficult challenge I face.

Analysis/Solution

There are a few things that may help you solve this problem. If your students are overly social, give them some structured time to talk to each other about whatever they would like. For example, you might set aside 2 minutes per class during which you will allow socializing with others. Another option is to use social time as a reward for being quiet while you are teaching and explaining new content. A third possibility is to give repeat violators instruction and content the day before class and to tell them that you may ask them to teach class the next day if they insist on interrupting or socializing while you are trying to instruct. Some teachers find it helpful to make periodic summarizing of content one of the class responsibilities. For example, after each 10-minute interval, ask students to review key details that were just explained. Finally, you might make cooperation part of your grading system. Ideally, two grades are earned: one for achievement and the other for effort and attitude. If this is not possible, then let your students know that up to 20% of their grade will be based on participation and cooperation.

Situation

I run an alternative education class with older students. Students try to sleep, lie on tables, steal from each other, argue, swear, and refuse to do any work. I need help!

Analysis/Solution

There are few easy answers here. You are dealing with students who have given up. Few, if any, believe that success is possible. Most of them probably see little connection between success in school and success in life.

Your first job is to be tough and not give up on them, because many of them have already given up on themselves. Be upfront with them and tell them that you know how much of a struggle school can be. Express to them in a dynamic way that you are sick and tired of treating them as prisoners (or animals, if that makes for a better analogy). Tell them:

> Your behavior tells me you have given up. I'm not sure I blame you since no one likes to think of themselves as stupid or incompetent, and I am sure that plenty of people along the way have helped you believe you are incapable. That makes me sad and mad. My bottom line is that I will not today, tomorrow, or ever give up on you. I will constantly remind you that you are capable by harassing you to do the work and by showing you that you can be and will be successful.

Have your students present themselves in class through photographs and artwork, and make it a daily goal to have fun with them. Keep an ongoing record of their progress that you can chart and share with each student. This is important because many tend to give up when things become difficult; they must see evidence of success and progress that came from previous efforts. Finally, if you find that none of these suggestions work well over a given period of time, you might implement a behavior modification program that identifies specific valued privileges that can be earned by the students in return for appropriate behavior.

Situation

I do not get anywhere near the administrative support that I need at school. When I send kids to the office, they usually come back worse than when they left my class. I get the sense that the administration

would rather me not send them any more kids. How can I get the administration to be more supportive concerning discipline issues?

Analysis/Solution

It is important to remember that administrators rarely know what has transpired when students show up at the office. I have yet to meet a student who gives a comprehensive summary of what led to the referral. When asked what happened, few if any students will answer with something similar to the following: "I was a disrespectful, unmotivated lump who used profanities when my teacher called on me." Most students make themselves look as innocent as possible and typically blame the teacher for the problem. Another problem is that the only thing that represents the teacher at this initial conference may be a hastily written referral with words such as "defiant, disobedient, unmotivated, insubordinate, and inappropriate." (Usually no one has the time to write a detailed referral in the middle of a class conflict.)

Let your administrators know that you plan to refer students very infrequently. Honestly, most administrators do not want to see referred students. Realistically, there is actually little they can do to fix most problems, and they become uncomfortable with teachers who expect nothing less than a perfectly behaved student returning from the office. Clearly understand and identify the goals that are likely to be met as a result of sending students to the administrators. It is generally much more manageable to ask for temporary relief (such as a minimum of 15 minutes without the annoying student in the classroom) rather than to expect major program changes. When major program change seems necessary to you, be sure to work through proper channels to ensure as much support for these changes as you can get. For example, have other professionals ready to support change through proper evaluations and prior efforts. Document your efforts and what you have done in an attempt to make matters better. It can also be very helpful for you to meet with administrators and suggest interventions that you would like to see them use because of your more personal knowledge of the student. One of the toughest times following a referral is the return of the student to class. Most students save face by looking as if nothing happened when they return. This is usually just a front. If you can ignore this pretense by welcoming the student back openly and in a friendly way, the escalation rapidly diminishes. Are you looking for some brief respite from the student or are you looking for the administrator to fix the situation? When possible, ask your administrator(s) to accompany the student back to class when the time is right. This will help ease a tough transition time.

Situation

Despite all the high-profile incidents of violence and the efforts to help our students understand that teasing and harassment can lead to violence, certain students continue to be teased. We have a clearly written school policy with consequences that prohibits verbal, sexual, and physical harassment, yet the problem continues. What else can be done?

Analysis/Solution

I am not sure that teasing and bullying behavior can ever be fully controlled. As we look around the world, there are many trouble spots in which one group of people derive and sustain power from bullying and diminishing the worth of others. Yet there is much that we can and need to do to make these behaviors objectionable to our students. It is correct to have a policy with enforcement procedures. As mentioned previously, in addition to a policy that might publicly emphasize particularly egregious incidents through consequences such as suspension and even filing police charges, adults need to confront bullying behaviors in a consistent, firm, and low-key way. In addition, the school's culture needs to ensure that students view this behavior as unacceptable and feel empowered to deal with violations. It is far more effective for six students to confront a violator with "we don't do that here" than it is for any single student to go it alone. It is also very important to work with victims. Most have been scarred by repeatedly being victimized and feel very incapable of doing much to influence what happens. They need help recapturing good feelings about who they are and what they can do. A few unwittingly send out verbal and nonverbal messages that encourage others to abuse them. These students can benefit from learning how to attract attention in less hostile ways.

Too often, bullying, harassment, and teasing are issues that capture a school's attention only after a high-profile incident of violence; attention to these issues rapidly fades soon after. Dealing successfully with this matter requires an ongoing, vigilant effort. When groups such as teachers and administrators, student council, and PTA are involved in ongoing initiatives to address bullying, harassment, and teasing, positive results usually occur and continue.

Situation

I am a substitute teacher, and I find that my biggest problem is maintaining classroom discipline. For some students, it seems as though my presence invites them to have a field day and do whatever they want. What can I do to be effective?

Analysis/Solution

As a substitute teacher, you have little if any time to get to know the students. There are some things you can do to prevent discipline problems, such as gaining the respect of your students and knowing effective strategies to handle problems when they occur. Here is a list of helpful suggestions:

- Develop your own list of rules and consequences that you can print on poster board and display in the room. You might meet in advance with the teacher or principal for help in designing enforceable, realistic consequences. Bring these rules with you whenever you teach.

- Tell students immediately that you plan to have an enjoyable day with them that includes important learning experiences designed by the regular classroom teacher. Tell them that you do not want to bore them with rules, but you want to make sure that everyone remains respectful during the day. Then share specifics based on the cardboard display. When you have finished, you might ask the students to choose one or two rules they want you to follow during the day that will best help them learn.

- Talk to the teacher(s) you will be substituting for on a regular or semi-regular basis, and express your strong desire to have him or her discuss with students the conduct that is expected of them when substitutes teach the class. If possible, come into class one day when the teacher is present and coteach a lesson—this will help you and the students get to know each other.

- Show up with a surplus of interesting "rainy day" activities that can be used to engage your students. These activities may have little or nothing to do with the subject, but they can succeed in getting everyone's attention. After beginning class with one or two of these activities, let the students know that when they have worked through the required lesson with proper behavior, a few more of these fun activities might be possible.

- Share one or two things about yourself that may be of interest to the students. Tell them that you look forward to treating them with respect during the day and that you will expect the same from them.

- Have fun. Show up with a positive, friendly attitude. Prepare at least one thing to do that you enjoy.

- Regular classroom teachers can offer help to the substitute teacher in a variety of ways. First, be sure that there is a list of important procedures for the substitute teacher to follow. Tell your students you expect them to show even more respect to the substitute teacher than is typically shown to you because the substitute is, after all, a visitor. Be sure to leave specific, detailed lesson plans that will enable the substitute to have a successful academic day. You might include tips that might help with certain students. Finally, call one or two especially difficult students the night before, and let them know that you will not be there the next day. Tell them who the substitute teacher will be (if this is known), and ask for their help in making sure that the day goes well. Tell them that you will be calling them the next night to follow up.

Many of the same intervention procedures described elsewhere in this book work just as well for substitute teachers as they do for regular teachers. It can be especially effective to respectfully yet firmly confront inappropriate behavior immediately by saying something such as, "I feel disrespected and that is not okay. I will expect proper behavior from this moment on. Thank you."

Situation

I teach music and find that some students who are apparently well-behaved in other classes see their time in my class as an opportunity to act up. Do you have any strategies that will help keep these students in line?

Analysis/Solution

Special area teachers such as those who teach music, art, and physical education often ask if there are any particular tips especially useful for them and their situations. Unfortunately, as most of these teachers know, many students do not value these subjects as much as they do the "core" academic subjects. Therefore, customary leverage strategies such as the use of grades and phone calls home tend to be less effective in special areas than they are in traditional academic classes. Further, art and music are performance subjects in which talent is usually quite obvious. Some students simply lack ability. Because the requirements for these classes often involve performance, it is not unusual for students who know that they lack talent to hide their inadequacies by either acting out or by becoming unmotivated. It is therefore particularly important for special area teachers to use a multitude of teaching strategies and to have performance requirements that even the least able student can attain.

Have frequent class performances in which every student has a role that is important to the success of the presentation. This involves the students and often prevents discipline problems. For example, instead of (or in addition to) a major concert before the holiday break and another at the end of the school year, have several smaller concerts so that students can display their progress on a more regular basis. Students with poor singing voices can be involved in lighting or taping, and students with little artistic talent might be responsible for arranging the show. It can be quite motivating and rewarding for even untalented students to see or hear evidence of success in their efforts. Try to create lessons that challenge all students—from the least to most talented. Keep in mind that performances do not have to be mega-events: You can have several groups serve as a willing audience, such as other classes, parents and grandparents, and senior citizens.

Situation

I have fewer problems with my students than I do with their parents. In my school, the parents are forever making excuses for their kids and demanding everything from me and virtually nothing from their children. I'm really stressed out because of this.

Analysis/Solution

Unfortunately, there are growing numbers of parents who think their children can do no wrong. Phone calls home for support often result in hearing accusations of blame. For example, a phone call to the parents of a student cheating on a test can easily turn into a demand from parents for proof, rather than an agreement from the parents to support the teacher by giving the student an appropriate consequence.

These parents do not realize that they are not helping their children. Kids who are continually rescued from their responsibilities grow up believing that they are entitled to success without adequate effort. Sadly, many capable kids become functionally unable to handle life's frustrations. It is therefore critically important that educators persist in demanding responsibility from our students, even when support from their parents is nonexistent.

When you know you are right, do not give in to the pressure from parents (and sometimes administrators) to be accommodating in order to avoid conflict. Although you should listen respectfully to the parental point of view, in the end you need to do what is educationally sound rather than what might be politically correct. Remember that being a good teacher is about teaching better behavior; it is not about placating the angry or reinforcing the irresponsible. Tell the parent:

> Thanks for your concern. Just like you, I want to be fair to your child. To excuse his actions would be to expect far less than he is capable of delivering. I really believe that if I didn't hold him accountable for cheating, I would be letting him down. I would worry that he would think not only that cheating is okay, but also that people like you and me do not believe he is capable unless he does cheat. I think too highly of your child to send him such a message, and I am sure you do as well. Since this is the

first time, I am going to just give him an F on the test and require a make-up test during detention rather than give him an in-school suspension that students caught cheating usually receive.

The following tips can help you establish and maintain a supportive relationship with difficult parents:

1. Try making two positive phone calls home before asking for help from administrators. The first call should come at the beginning of the school year to make an introduction:

    > Hi *(address them as "Mr. or Mrs. So-and-so")*, my name is _____, and I will be your child's teacher this year. I wanted to call and let you know what it usually takes for students to be successful in my class. I try very hard to meet each student's needs, so I was hoping you could give me some information about your child that could help. I'd like to know three things that your child likes to do, three things your child likes best about school, and three things your child likes least about school. Please tell me anything you feel I should know about your child that could help me to make school a successful experience for *(him or her)*.

    The second phone call should be made within the first month after the student has done something warranting positive notice: "I'm calling to let you know that Lori has been making good progress in reading and has been doing a nice job looking out for other children." It can be especially powerful to make a phone call like this to parents at work. Not only will the parents feel good, they are likely to tell everyone else around them about the phone call, making you and your school look good. Phone calls such as these set a foundation for support when you need it.

2. Do not attack, criticize, or put down the child. When parents are made to feel they have failed, they will be hurt and angry. Defuse their anger by thanking them for caring enough about their child to become angry with you: "Your child is very lucky to have a parent who cares enough about him to become angry at me." Begin sharing your concerns with words such as, "I feel badly that you are so upset about Ron, and I look forward to finding ways for him to be more successful in this class with your help. What do you think we can do to make sure this doesn't happen again?"

3. Ask questions in an involved way, revealing your sincere interest in the student. Ask intelligent and intuitive questions because you care and want to know as much as possible so you can be helpful. Try to determine the parents' approach toward discipline in an effort to answer the following questions:

   • What, if anything, does your child do at home that requires discipline?

   • What methods/techniques work best for you in the management of your child's behavior?

   • What, if anything, concerning your child's behaviors do you find unacceptable but you can't seem to have much success changing?

4. If parents cross the line and speak to you offensively, say to them calmly and assertively, "Please do not talk to me in that way. I will not talk to you in such a manner, and I would never talk to your child or any of the children in that way. Thank you."

5. Keep your focus on two goals: *success* and *responsibility*. Let parents know that you are willing to do whatever it takes to accomplish these two goals.

10 Concluding Thoughts

Too many students come to school lacking the social skills and respect for others necessary for good teaching and learning to occur. Too often, fine educators lose their enthusiasm and energy for teaching because of difficult students who do not care, will not work, and refuse to cooperate. Rather than becoming angry or burning out, there is much we can do every day to promote positive behavior without consuming large amounts of instructional time. When we establish a values-based classroom that integrates prevention and intervention strategies dealing with the causes of misbehavior, we will gain much more time to teach and create a much healthier learning climate for our students. *MORE What Do I Do When . . . ? Powerful Strategies to Promote Positive Behavior* provides a sensible framework that guides educators, administrators, and staff toward effective ways of:

- Welcoming students
- Developing effective rules and consequences
- Promoting responsibility
- Inspiring motivation for learning

This book prepares educators for challenging moments by showing not just *what* to say and do, but also *why* to say and do it. Being a good teacher or administrator has never been easy, but it is even more challenging when we must deal with increasing numbers of poorly prepared students, a litany of social problems, and parents who are too eager to blame others for their own shortcomings. Being effective requires that we refuse to give up and that we use practical strategies that can change even our most difficult students. By empowering and reinvigorating ourselves through the numerous ideas, strategies, and methods suggested in this book, we can increase our influence and our happiness.

I invite you to share with me the strategies, tips, and ideas that you find effective with your students so that we can continue to help each other find ways of making positive differences in the lives of the children with whom we work. You can contact me at Discipline Associates, P.O. Box 20481, Rochester, NY 14602; (800) 772-5227 or allen.mendler@disciplineassociates.com.

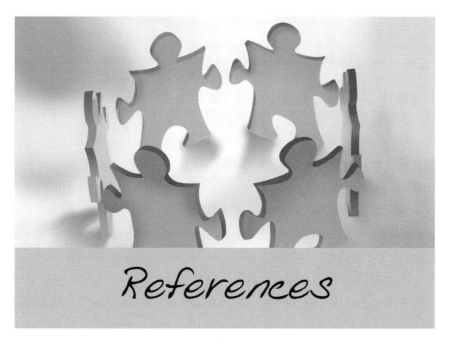

References

Brendtro, L. K., Brokenleg, M., & Van Bockern, S. (1997, 2002). *Reclaiming youth at risk: Our hope for the future.* Bloomington, IN: Solution Tree (formerly National Educational Service).

Canfield, J., & Hansen, M. V. (1993). *Chicken soup for the soul.* Deerfield Beach, FL: Health Communications.

Charles, C. M. (2002). *Building classroom discipline* (7th ed.). Boston, MA: Allyn & Bacon.

Coloroso, B. (2003). *The bully, bullied and the bystander: From preschool to high school—how parents and teachers can help break the cycle of violence.* New York: HarperCollins Publishers.

Covey, S. (1989). *The seven habits of highly effective people.* New York: Simon & Schuster.

Curwin, R. (2003). *Making good choices.* Thousand Oaks, CA: Corwin.

Curwin, R., & Mendler, A. (1997). *As tough as necessary: A discipline with dignity approach to countering aggression, hostility, and violence.* Alexandria, VA: Association for Supervision and Curriculum Development.

Curwin, R., & Mendler, A. (1988, 1999). *Discipline with dignity* (Rev. ed). Alexandria, VA: Association for Supervision and Curriculum Development.

Curwin, R., & Mendler, A. (1999, 2007). Discipline with dignity for challenging youth. Bloomington, IN: Solution Tree (formerly National Educational Service).

Dwyer, K., & Skiba, R. (1999). School violence: Listening to the students. *NASP Communique, 28*(2), 4. (retrieved May 18, 2004). Available at www.nasponline.org/publications/cq282violence.html

Elgin, S. H. (1980). *The gentle art of verbal self-defense.* Huntsville, AR: Dorsett Press.

Evans, R. (2002). Family matters. *Education Week, 21*(37), 48.

Gardner, H. (2000). *Intelligence reframed: Multiple intelligence for the 21st Century.* New York: Basic Books.

Glasser, W. (1986). *Control theory in the classroom.* New York: Harper & Row.

Goodlad, J. (1984). *A place called school: Promise for the future.* New York: The McGraw-Hill Companies.

Hoover, J. H., & Olsen, G. W. (2001). *Teasing and harassment: The frames and scripts approach for teachers and parents.* Bloomington, IN: Solution Tree (formerly National Educational Service).

Hyman, I. A. (1996, 1997). *School discipline and school violence.* Needham Heights, MA: Allyn & Bacon.

Kindlon, D. (2003). *Too much of a good thing: Raising children of character in an indulgent age.* New York: Miramax Books.

Meichenbaum, D. (1977). *Cognitive behavior modification.* New York: Plenum.

Mendler, A. (1991). *Smiling at yourself: Educating young children about stress and self-esteem.* Santa Cruz, CA: ETR Associates.

Mendler, A. (1992, 2007). *What do I do when . . . ? How to achieve discipline with dignity in the classroom.* Bloomington, IN: Solution Tree (formerly National Educational Service).

Mendler, A. (1997). *Power struggles: Successful techniques for educators.* Rochester, NY: Discipline Associates.

Mendler, A. (2001). *Connecting with students.* Alexandria, VA: Association for Supervision and Curriculum Development.

References

Muhlenbruck, L., Cooper, H., Nye, B., & Lindsay, J. J. (2000). Homework and achievement: Explaining the different relations at the elementary and secondary school levels. *Social Psychology of Education 4,* 295–317.

Public Agenda. (2004). *Teaching interrupted: Do discipline policies in today's public schools foster the common good?* New York: Author.

Sagor, R. (2003). *Motivating students and teachers in an era of standards.* Alexandria, VA: Association for Supervision and Curriculum Development.

Smith, R. (2003). *Conscious classroom management.* San Rafael, CA: Conscious Teaching Publications.

U.S. Secret Service. (2000, October). *Safe school initiative: An interim report on the prevention of targeted violence in schools.* Washington, D.C.: National Threat Assessment Center, U.S. Secret Service.

Whitaker, T., & Fiore, D. J. (2001). *Dealing with difficult parents: And with parents in difficult situations.* Larchmont, New York: Eye On Education.

Make the Most of Your Professional Development Investment

Let Solution Tree (formerly National Educational Service) schedule time for you and your staff with leading practitioners in the areas of:

- **Professional Learning Communities** with Richard DuFour, Robert Eaker, Rebecca DuFour, and associates
- **Effective Schools** with associates of Larry Lezotte
- **Assessment *for* Learning** with Rick Stiggins and associates
- **Crisis Management and Response** with Cheri Lovre
- **Classroom Management** with Lee Canter and associates
- **Discipline With Dignity** with Richard Curwin and Allen Mendler
- **PASSport to Success** (parental involvement) with Vickie Burt
- **Peacemakers** (violence prevention) with Jeremy Shapiro

Additional presentations are available in the following areas:

- At-Risk Youth Issues
- Bullying Prevention/Teasing and Harassment
- Team Building and Collaborative Teams
- Data Collection and Analysis
- Embracing Diversity
- Literacy Development
- Motivating Techniques for Staff and Students

Solution Tree

304 W. Kirkwood Avenue
Bloomington, IN 47404-5131
(812) 336-7700
(800) 733-6786 (toll-free number)
FAX (812) 336-7790
email: info@solution-tree.com
www.solution-tree.com

Discipline With Dignity for Challenging Youth
Allen N. Mendler and Richard L. Curwin
Create positive change in your most challenging students with the help of proven, practical strategies found in this resource.   **BK086**

The Four Keys to Effective Classroom and Behavior Management
Richard L. Curwin and Allen N. Mendler
Explore four skill areas essential to establishing a safe, supportive learning environment. In this video series, Curwin and Mendler demonstrate research-based strategies that work.   **VIF093**

What Do I Do When . . . ? How to Achieve Discipline With Dignity in the Classroom
Allen N. Mendler
Understand the principles that place dignity at the core of classroom management, and explore what motivates misbehavior. This book also provides unique, effective strategies for making a positive impact on school-wide discipline.   **BKF230**

Motivating Students Who Don't Care: Successful Techniques for Educators
Allen N. Mendler
Proven strategies and five effective processes empower you to reawaken motivation in students who aren't prepared, don't care, and won't work.   **BKF102**

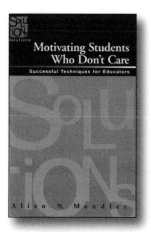

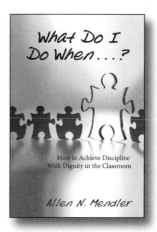